Don Willcox

Hmong Folklife

Don Willcox

Hmong Natural Association of North Carolina
1986

This book is dedicated to our new roof

the
United
States
Of
America

Long may it shelter the house of Hmong

Table of Contents

Credits

Book Design, Layout, Paste-up, and Direction: Robert Oldham
Cover Illustration: Rhea Rose Ormond
Black and White Line Illustrations: Thongsay Kue
Black and White Photographs: Don Willcox and Jack Lauterer
Color Photographs: Don Willcox
Typesetting: Typo-Repro Service, Inc.
Printing: J & M Printing
Binding: Copple House Books
Copyright: Don Willcox

About the Author

Don Willcox is the author of 20 other books, including several titles within the visual arts, seven books of poetry, and the widely acclaimed book, *The Ribbon - a Celebration of Life*. His book on the design environment of Finland received the Finnish National Book Award. Mr. Willcox is a National Endowment for the Arts recipient, a frequent traveler in Asia, and has spent long periods of his life abroad. He lives in a hand-made house at Penland, North Carolina, writes regularly for a number of arts publications, and coordinates an outreach program for destitute children in Nepal.

Preface

As author of this book, it would be entirely presumptuous to at any time imply or suggest to a reader that this book represents the "whole" picture of Hmong folklife. On the contrary, with obviously limited funds and resources, we have barely scratched the surface of an incredibly rich subject matter. What the book does try to do, however, is to introduce America's newest neighbor in the hope that discovery will be ongoing. In years to come, the Hmong must learn to write about themselves. They must use the advent of written language, ink, paper, and democracy to record and communicate as a culture.

Some of my Hmong friends have seen so much of me in recent months that they affectionately accuse me of newly formed high cheekbones, Hmong eyes, and a noodle and rice personality. On my part, and after witnessing their dramatic Americanization so intimately, I often counter by reminding my Hmong friends about their "hamburger and fries" tummies.

Just prior to publication, I accompanied a Hmong family on a visit to the Cherokee Indian Reservation. It was full summer. My usually lily white skin was reasonably tan. As we stood at a Cherokee agency for fishing licenses, a full-blooded Cherokee clerk asked us to complete a space on the permit form that called for a designation of "RACE". Both my Hmong friend and I began to giggle. We looked at each other. "Officially", he was supposed to be "yellow", I was supposed to be "white", and our clerk was supposed to be "red". In actual reality, I was the darkest of the three, my Hmong friend was white, and the Cherokee could have easily advertised ragu-sauce.

So it is with this book...it might look like an "authority", but it is not! It is a step. Only a step, and a step that is made without a Hmong publishing tradition, and without an accumulated Hmong recorded history. What follows is a blend between word of mouth and limited, available research material. From what appears, there may well be differences of opinion, or memory. Some of the Hmong remember it one way... some remember it another. Some agree...some don't. Unfortunately there is no great Hmong "scholar in the sky" to turn to for absolute authority. We did the best we could, and apologize for mistakes.

Foreword

One bright ember in the afterglow of America's growth as a nation has been its continuing role as a safe harbor for many of the world's oppressed people. Each year, thousands emigrate to America. They learn its language, find constructive employment, adjust to our ways, and become a contributing part of this nation. Very often, during the press to "Americanize", many of the "old ways" are too quickly discarded as obsolete. The immigrant feels considerable pressure to "blend", to assume the plumage of Uncle Sam, and to disappear into the crowd in order not to stand out. Too often, our wonderful "new" Americans allow rich cultural heritages to simply waft away, sacrificed to a proliferation of Lee jeans, fast foods, ghetto blasters, and football games.

The time for the image of America as the world's "melting pot" is long past. We are, in fact, a *mosaic*! We are a collection of tiles...individually colored, glazed, and fired. Today is a period in which we owe it to ourselves to celebrate the harmonious blending of our differences.

This book exists as a challenge to the Hmong in America to preserve the beauty of their culture within our own. The contributions of all of us, both individually and collectively, have added to our national maturity. We obviously have much to learn from the Hmong. We embrace this opportunity to share.

Sandra Epperson, Executive Director
McDowell Arts and Crafts Association
Marion, North Carolina

Introduction

In 1979, in the San Fransisco Bay area, I was first introduced to the Hmong through a psychologist friend who was concerned about Hmong problems of cultural adjustment. Later, I had a more direct and personal connection with the Hmong through the John Michael Kohler Arts Center in Sheboygan, Wisconsin when they sponsored the May, 1985 National Conference of Hmong Traditional Artists. My association with Hmong has shifted my perspective, rotated my vision, and opened new direction.

The lessons so poignantly impressed upon me by the Hmong have been those of determination, core value, and spirituality. As we, in the contemporary art (and other) world, compete to refine our products, professionalize our presentations, broaden our markets, and educate our audiences ... we shift, by degrees, away from the "spirit" of the object we're making. Our contemporary object world tends to lose touch with the spirituality of the "gift" in the sense of personal, direct involvement with the process.

The notion of "artist" as understood in a western, modernist culture does not exist in Hmong language or cultural experience. In the traditional life of the Hmong, everyone shares a creative, object-making impulse. The desire to decorate and to communicate through color and symbolism is deeply integrated into daily experience. Art is not a specialty for specialists.

The notion of "time" is also very differently understood by the Hmong. A time-intensive effort is not thought of in terms of its monetary value, or in terms of profit and loss. "Time" is much more perceived as one of the normal, essential ingredients required of each individual's investment in life...a way to express caring...a way of touching another human skin.

I once asked an aging Hmong woman how she had managed to find the time to accomplish all the stitchery in the "flower cloths" used by her family. The old woman replied that when storms passed over the fields in Laos, she would temporarily sit under a broad-leafed plant protected from rain and stitch. She was, after all, investing in the protection and celebration of her family with each stitch.

These fine people have enriched my thinking, and I have, in turn, found opportunities to translate their thinking into my own life. Just last year, for example, in response to the Hmong tradition to prepare burial garments during life in order to be properly identified as Hmong in the "new life", I wove a piece which I entitled "Funeral Coat". I later wrote about this piece as follows: "...I have woven a white plastic coat to say I am who I am. You can see through these clothes to my body and yet I shimmer to reflect light. I throw in a little plaid with gold threads to connect with my Scottish ancestors plus a stream for the fish on their way to the great ocean in the skies. I think the angels will smile when they see me wearing this coat".

Jean McLaughlin, Director
Visual Arts Section
North Carolina Arts Council

Historical Synopsis

The Word "Hmong" A controversy exists over the meaning of the word "Hmong". There are those who insist that the word means "free men" while others (especially lexicographers) define the word to mean "tendon, artery, cord, or seam". What we do know for certain, is that the word "Hmong" is used by the Laotian-American Hmong people to describe themselves. In English, the word is pronounced with a silent "H".

In southeast Asia, China, and other parts of the world, the Hmong are referred to as "Meo" or "Miao". According to Dr. Amy Catlin, early Chinese records in the *Book of Documents* from the 3rd century B.C. refer to a people

"Miao" from north Thailand wearing traditional clothing.

1

called "Miao" who lived in the Hunan province of China as early as 2255 B.C. Dr. Catlin writes that the word "Miao", when written in Chinese characters, forms a compound that means "sprouts, seedlings, or sprouting grain".

Within the Laotian-American community, we do know that the words "Meo", or "Miao" have negative connotations. Our Hmong do not want to be called by either name. For them, both names conjure unpleasant memories. Reports indicate that in Laos, the terms were used within a derogatory context to mean "cat-like", and actually used as a slur or "cat call". By chiding a person and calling out the word "meow" (as in the sound made by a cat), the respondent was being deliberately harassed.

Hmong History   A recent, 1985 publication by the Nationality Press of Beijing, China, and entitled *Clothings and Ornaments of China's Miao People* indicates that Hmong roots stem from the provinces of south China. According to a 1982 Chinese Population Census, more than 5 million "Miao" people still live in the southern provinces of Guizhou, Hunan, Yunnan, Sichuan, Guangdong, and Hubei, as well as the Autonomous Region of Guangxi Zhuang. The Census indicates that a concentration of 2,588,277 "Miao" people still live in Guizhou province and that some 761,754 "Miao" still live in the province of Hunan where the *Book of Documents* referred to the "Miao" presence from 2255 B.C.

The Hmong have always been an ethnic minority, and have always had to fit themselves within a majority political system. Being an "underdog", a "maverick", or a "well behaved guest in a dominant majority" is as normal to a Hmong as breathing. Over the centuries, the Hmong have been conquered, divided, forced to adapt to someone else's rule, exiled, and plundered so often that it would require a separate volume just to keep track of the exchanges. Western historians have labelled the Hmong as being "semi-nomadic" without asking why this is, and without regard to the fact that as a cultural minority forever being pushed around…these folks might have wandered from place to place for no other reason than that they were simply looking for a place to settle where they would no longer be culturally abused. It is clear that they did not elect the "semi-nomadic" lifestyle because they were restless, or "foot loose". On the contrary, the historian who has never known what it feels like to be a perpetual minority, is in no position to slap labels on an entire ethnic culture numbering in the millions. Historians also tend to refer to the Hmong as a "tribe". This seems to us to be a ridiculous use of the term. We prefer to call a culture comprising millions of individuals, a "people".

Hmong are referred to as *swidden* (slash and burn) agriculturalists. As they migrated from south China into Laos, Vietnam, Burma, and Thailand, they had to adapt to changing climatic conditions, soil conditions, geography, and growing seasons. In semi-tropical and tropical environments, they often had to deal with

2

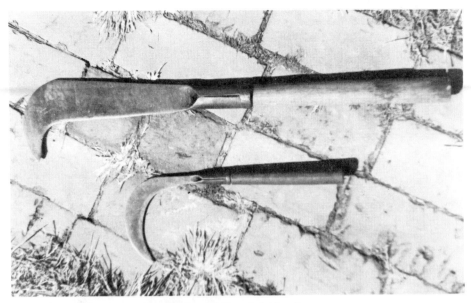
Traditional Hmong field tools.

an undergrowth that was so prolific that it tended to close in around you as you watched. Slash and burn provided ash to fertilize the soil, space for crops, and an access to a pattern of crop rotation. Unlike western mono-planting, where we tend to grow one crop at a time, or one crop in sections...the Hmong tend to mix their plantings with an almost uncanny sensitivity for companion planting. These folks know how to grow edible grains, herbs, fodder, vegetables, fibers used to produce cloth, and other growing plants that contribute to a self-sufficient lifestyle.

During the Ming dynasty (14th to 17th centuries), there was such extreme abrasion between the Chinese and the "Miao", that a 9 foot fortified wall was built some 120 miles in length along the Kweichow eastern border to protect and separate the two peoples. Friction with the "Miao" minority continued to erupt in skirmishes and major outbreaks during the first half of the 18th century, with the "Miao" always suffering heavy losses. Dr. Amy Catlin reports "Miao" losses between 1734-1737 at 17,000 killed in action, 12,000 villages burned (leaving only 388 villages standing), 27,000 taken as prisoner, and half of these promptly executed.

Dr. Catlin reports that for the next nearly fifty years, there was relative peace, but then another so-called "Miao rebellion" in opposition to harsh restrictions began to account for large scale migrations southward into parts of

In Laos, before the exodus.

southeast Asia, especially Laos, Vietnam, and Thailand. This migration, however, did not alleviate the ever present dark shadow of minority existence. The "push and pull" to align Hmong energies with non Hmong power struggles continued. In Vietnam, the Hmong resisted Japanese occupation during the Second World War, then resisted the Viet Minh from 1946-1954, and finally aligned themselves in large numbers with the French "Groupements Mixtes de Commandos Aeroportes" until they were promised three autonomous zones by the Viet Minh in the region bordering China.

Similar "push-pull" conditions existed for the Hmong who migrated into northern Laos. There were conflicts with the Lao, the Khmou, as well as inter clan conflicts within the Hmong. Only two years after the 1949 Laotian indepen-

4

North Carolina Hmong New Year, Hillcrest Elementary School, Morganton, N.C.

(L) A young Kue family member prepares soft drinks. (R) A New Year's table of culinary delights. 5

"Dig in", Hmong style.

A Laotian-American Hmong family, part Asian, part "western".

The only adult male in traditional clothing has no lack of attention.

No wonder he was overwhelmed with attention!

Another kind of headdress.

dence, the "Pathet Lao" and the Vietnamese and Khmer liberation movements signed an agreement which aided the "Pathet Lao" in controlling most of the mountainous regions of northern Laos. When the French pulled out of Vietnam in 1954, the gap was filled by American aid, not only to Laos, but also to Vietnam and Cambodia. During President Kennedy's term, the United States decided to send "special forces" into the area in order to train guerillas. The Hmong became the central focus of this training…and thus began the in-depth American-Hmong connection.

Inasmuch as the Hmong were segregated from the regular Laotian military troops because of their unpopular minority status, the U.S. Central Intelligence Agency, working through the Agency for International Development (U.S.A.I.D.), took over the logistical support and administration of the Hmong troops. General Vang Pao's Hmong troops performed invaluable service to the United States. As Americans know only too well, and too painfully, the whole roof fell in despite massive U.S. support. In February, 1973, the government of the Laotian King Souvanna Phouma formed a coalition government with the "Pathet Lao", the U.S.A.I.D. discontinued its "aid to refugees", and by early 1975 it was all over for the United States in Laos. Hmong casualties were extraordinary. The Hmong culture was temporarily devastated. Tens of thousands of Hmong people were killed, wounded, homeless, endangered, and left dangling.

The Hmong began to leave Laos in great numbers by April, 1975. They had supported the United States, but America was forced to pull out. For the Hmong to have remained in Laos, especially for those who had aided the United States, would have been tantamount to suicide. So they left! They headed for Thailand. Hmong of all ages. Some of them with special United States military connections were flown out, or were able to "hitch" partial rides. The overwhelming majority, however, walked out…children, parents, and grand-parents. To avoid detection, many of them hid by day and walked by night.

The Mekong river runs the border between Laos and Thailand. There are times, particularly during monsoons, when the Mekong is a raging torrent of water trapped between finite banks. Men, women, children, infants, and the aged…all had to cross the Mekong river, often wading across in the dark. Whatever was left over from their former lives, they carried on their backs. It has been estimated that between one-quarter to one-half million people (mostly Hmong) made their way from Laos into the refugee camps of Thailand.

Once in Thailand, the United States, as well as the United Nations and several other countries offered assistance to these displaced people. Assistance took the form of food, medicine, clothing, and resettlement. It seems fair to say that Thailand, and most "western" nations, were unprepared to deal with such vast numbers of departing people, especially when one considers that most of the refugees were a closely knit ethnic minority with a common language, and

8

cultural heritage. Under these extraordinary circumstances of refugee camps bulging at the seams, "western" nations did what they could.

The Hmong had to be split up. No single plot of global real estate was large enough, or immediately accessible enough to accomodate this many people. Hmong were consequently scattered and sent to France, Germany, Canada, Australia, and the United States. Regional groups, kin groups, and even family groups were split apart and resettled as logistical solutions, rather than as cultural solutions. The physical closeness that had sustained these ethnic refugees for over 4,000 years of recorded history was being shattered by reason of emergency and necessity.

Of the 60,000 Hmong who eventually made it to the United States, they too were split apart and resettled at great distances from one another and in vastly contrasting geographies. Because it was impossible to accept them as a single group, we resettled them along the seaside of Rhode Island, on the plains of the midwest, in the mountains of the far west, on the northwest Pacific coast, in the Bible Belt of the south, and in the central valleys of California.

In the throes of emergency and necessity, America accepted a refugee people who had rarely, if ever seen snow, and we resettled them in states where below

Thongsay Kue

Backpack baskets - on left the strap is made from water buffalo - on right, from bamboo.

zero winter temperatures were absolutely normal. We resettled a mountain people in areas where there were no mountains, and we often placed a rural, self-sufficient people in the midst of public housing units within major, complex, and often hostile American cities.

Within these logistical resettlement problems and numbers...there were real, individual Hmong people...people with feelings, fears, and sorrows. Within an abrupt condensation of time, the circumstances imposed by history demanded that these people endure and survive incredible change. They had lost everything that had ever been dear to them...loved ones, homes, villages, kin groups, and country. Upon arrival in the United States, they were, as if propelled ahead in a time warp of several centuries. Not only were they confronted with an abrupt change of language, food, climate, religion, social mores, architecture, clothing, and geography, but they were also, for the first time, confronting telephones, electricity, traffic jams, fast foods, regular indoor plumbing...the complete myriad of 20th century American technology which the rest of us had long been taking for granted. Change had to be learned, and learned quickly.

Only those of us who have been in similar, confrontational readjustment situations can begin to understand the depth of what any of this really feels like on the inside. It involves nearly a total transformation of our familiar, everyday environment...sounds, smells, movements, spaces, and even those daily events we take for granted, such as the simple recognition of familiar birds, trees, and flowers. Obviously, changes as drastic as the changes experienced by Hmong refugees, can generate fear, confusion, loneliness, and the terrible, dull ache one feels at the pit of the stomach from lamenting so very much from a life that has been forever left behind. It is the ache of every black slave, every displaced person, and the all too familiar immigrant ache on which much of this country was founded.

Although readjustment among the younger generation of Hmong has been almost instantaneous, many of the middle and older generations still feel shy, vulnerable, and tentative. The passing of time is, however, a period of recovery and fresh perspective. The Hmong are quick to discover their new country, particularly their freedom of choice. Like other Americans who decide they don't like the snow of the midwest, the long winters of the north, or the confusion of the city...the Hmong move to "greener" pastures. In the end, and like the rest of us, they'll make their own choices.

In preparing this text, I asked Dr. Amy Catlin to try to recall anecdotes that underline the ongoing struggle of refugee resettlement where the individual who is familiar with his or her own culture, invests such prolific energies to understand the ways and vernacular of an adopted culture. Dr. Catlin remembers the following story: Soon after she founded the *Center for Hmong Lore* in Providence, Rhode Island, one of her Hmong collaborators, with typical tact and restraint,

Traditional Hmong knives.

finally felt the time had come to ask Dr. Catlin an important question on behalf of the group. The collaborator approached Dr. Catlin and asked: "Dr. Amy, we are so very happy with the new Center and with all of its activities for our Hmong, but the time has finally come to ask you, who is this Hmong *Lord of the Center?*" Despite all good intentions, Dr. Catlin had chosen an imperfect name for the Providence Center. She had certainly intended that the center be a repository for Hmong "lore", but she had not intended it to offer salvation!

Another anecdote which underlines the same struggle involves an elderly Hmong woman who arrived at JFK International Airport directly from Thailand. Because of her age, an airport attendant courteously ushered her into an elevator in order to save climbing a flight of steps to Immigration. Once the elevator doors had closed automatically, and as the cubicle began its ascent, the old Hmong woman graciously assumed she had somehow "passed away" and was certainly on her way to heaven. Such is the inheritance of a refugee!

Ethnic Subgroups

Upon the publication of *Clothings and Ornaments of China's Miao People,* Nationality Press, Beijing, 1985, it is now visually evident that the Hmong or "Miao" people, did in fact, divide themselves into many subgroups. Previous researchers had recorded frequent references to subgroups, but stories were often fraught with contradiction and inconsistency. Most of our American knowledge had been passed along by Laotian Hmong. They differentiated between the subgroups by the color or pattern of their traditional clothing, such as White, Green (Blue), Black, Red, Striped, Flowery Hmong, and so forth. The recent Chinese publication confirms many subgroups.

Many of our Laotian-American Hmong recite stories that attribute clothing variations to Chinese authorities. According to the stories, the Chinese deliberately imposed variations in an attempt to divide the "Hmong house against itself", or in other words, to split the Hmong apart as a unified people. We do not know whether these stories are fact or fiction, but we do know that dialects exist within the Hmong language, and that there are both custom and costume variations. It seems plausible that these variations might just as easily be attributed to kin group conflicts, geographic separation, or even human idiosyncrasy. We do know that the Hmong were spread out over vast areas of south China and southeast Asia. It seems only reasonable that at least regional differences would eventually evolve.

At any rate, most Laotian-American Hmong divide themselves into two major groups...either White Hmong (hmoob dawb), or Green (Blue) Hmong (hmoob ntsuab). The Hmong who have settled in North Carolina also fall within these two subgroups. Sources suggest that the Green (Blue) Hmong tended to live in the north of Laos, speaking a northern dialect, whereas the White Hmong tended to live in the south of Laos, speaking a southern dialect.

The North Carolina Hmong

The first refugee Hmong in North Carolina arrived in 1976, directly from camps in Thailand. Their arrival, in large measure, was due to the compassion and foresight of Catholic Social Services in Charlotte. The first Hmong family arrived quietly, and without much fanfare.

Our Lady of the Angels parish in Marion, North Carolina, a member parish within the Charlotte diocese, heard about the Hmong arrival and offered a sponsorship of their own - once again, a quiet affair - a Hmong family arriving in a small, foothills community. Hardly anyone took notice. Life went on as usual.

Rev. Allen G. McKinney and Associate Pastor Don Guffey (far left) pose outside the Garden Creek Baptist Church with members of the recent Marion refugee Hmong community.

13

But then, early in 1979, Reverend Allen G. McKinney, pastor of the Garden Creek Baptist Church in Marion, changed everything. Reverend McKinney, a 6 foot 4 inch barrel-chested preacher who looks like he could wrestle a bear as well as preach a sermon, sat watching a television documentary about the plight of homeless Hmong. McKinney was so deeply moved with compassion that he found himself soaked with tears. He knew there were already a couple of Hmong families in the area...they were the lucky ones...the documentary made it quite clear that thousands more remained on "hold" in Thai refugee camps. Reverend McKinney decided to put words into action. He told his congregation how he felt and suggested that they could all do something about it. Garden Creek Baptist Church responded with a commitment to take action and to begin immediate sponsorship.

When the first Garden Creek Hmong family was scheduled to arrive, Rev. McKinney was in bed with the flu. Not knowing quite what to expect, he sent his Associate Pastor to the Charlotte airport. While the Associate stood waiting, no less than seven Hmong descended from the plane - grandparents, parents, and children - an entire extended family of 3 generations! For a brief moment of awkwardness, everyone stood looking at one another, but then the moment passed. Eight people then piled into the church van and headed down the road...a scene similar to one which was then taking place all over America...tiny groups of surviving Hmong refugees...clutching sparse possessions...having no idea where they were or where they were headed...a destination and future unknown...frightened to death on the one hand, excited by the promise of good times on the other...and always trusting. Oh how the Hmong trusted!

Marion, with a population of about 4,000 souls, is the largest community in McDowell County. It rests against the spine of the massive Black Mountains and is only a short drive from Mt. Mitchell, the highest peak east of the Rockies. Marion is very much a "main street" community with one major commercial thoroughfare, several cross streets, a couple of shopping streets, a good flea market, a technical college, a number of low-profile industries, very little sympathy for labor unions, and an abundance of churches. For a northerner, Marion would nearly perfectly fit the stereotyped prejudice of southern, Bible-belt conservatism. But yet, in reality, here was the exact same Marion, by virtue of its religious community, actually hosting and even soliciting Asian refugees.

And Hmong refugees, in fact, did continue to come in increasing numbers - some of them directly from the camps in Thailand, and others from across the United States in the wave of "secondary resettlement"...which really meant that the Hmong were making their own choices apart from the U.S. government. Reverend McKinney's task as a negotiator between a pained refugee group on the one hand, and a somewhat bewildered local community on the other hand became more and more important.

14

A mixed congregation, the Garden Creek Baptist Church.

Obviously, not everything was always "peaches and cream". A lot of stretching and compromise took place in Marion...also a large measure of understanding! Asian faces, foreign tongues, and unfamiliar clothing began to be commonplace in both Marion and nearby Morganton. As numbers of Hmong increased, the rumors and questions also increased. Letters-to-the-Editor began to appear in the *McDowell News* and the *McDowell Express*. Typical of what happened in many parts of the United States, Marion residents began to complain that the Hmong might take away local jobs, cannibalize welfare, usurp rental property, and God forbid...intermarry with locals. There were questions expressed about why the Hmong were in Marion in the first place, why the Hmong always seemed to have so many children, and a general confusion about the role the Hmong played during the Vietnam War...were they our friends, or were they our enemies? The controversy at one time even reached the level of the County Commissioners. Two of them in fact voted against continuing support for the Hmong. These Commissioners were, however, in the minority.

As the Hmong settled in, as they began to make positive contributions to the local economy, earn the trust and respect of area employers, become home owners, and prove themselves over and over as excellent caretakers of public housing...the questions and the controversy quieted down.

Rev. Allen G. McKinney at his desk.

Pat Jobe, a reporter for the *McDowell Express*, published an "Editor's Opinion" on September 10th, 1980 wherein he summarized the controversy as: "one side convinced that the opposing County Commissioners were heroic guardians of local jobs, while Reverend McKinney was obviously a bleeding-hearted preacher without the good sense to see the possible dangers of so many Hmong in McDowell County". Jobe went on to write that: "the other side may pitch the Commissioners into a dungeon reserved for the hard-hearted, while lifting McKinney next to the saints". Jobe concluded that: "the Hmong are proving to be assets to McDowell County and our local economy. They are working, paying taxes, and spending their earnings in local businesses. Many do need assistance when they arrive, but they work quickly to gain financial independence. Only two of them smoke, and none drink. America is going to rebound economically. Only here in the fresh air of freedom can ingenuity, work, and resources combine to stimulate new growth, more jobs, and more opportunities. As good times return, as our economy begins to rise, we will be glad that thrifty Hmong are at our sides, pulling their weight, raising strong families, and maintaining the values which make McDowell a great place to live".

At one point during the peak of resettlement, close to 750 Hmong had been resettled in the immediate, McDowell-Burke County area. Reverend McKinney's resolve remained undaunted in spite of occasional criticism, and in spite of one attempt (which fizzled) by the Ku Klux Klan to rally at McKinney's church.

Being the pivot point for refugee resettlement involved much more than only moral support. It involved fund raising (Rev. McKinney called fund raising a "love offering"), and local church members were also many times called upon to donate or scrounge large quantities of clothing, furniture, and other household goods. Reverend McKinney recalls that the outpouring of compassion was enormous. In retrospect, he considers it an honor to have participated in an experience which immeasureably enriched McDowell and Burke Counties. Obviously, northern skeptics and pundits don't know nearly as much as they think they know about the south and its people. In a space of only ten short years, McDowell County and the State of North Carolina have gone from accepting their first Hmong refugees to today, celebrating a North Carolina Hmong presence with the publication of this book.

Hmong Natural Association Of N.C., Inc.

As the number of Hmong in North Carolina grew into a stable community, there was an accompanying need for what essentially amounts to a Hmong "council" to oversee its own affairs, and to represent the Hmong in their communication with local, State, and Federal officials. The Hmong Natural Association of North Carolina was consequently incorporated on September 3, 1980. Incorporation signatures were Vang Xia Pao Ly and Cheu Vang. The Association was established as a non-profit, tax-exempt institution. Its immediate and long term goals included resettlement assistance, education, and the promotion and preservation of Hmong culture.

The Association includes a Board of Directors, a number of Executive Board officers, Special Advisors, and several employees - both full and part time. Because of the structure of Hmong society, the Hmong Natural Association is thus far entirely a male institution. Females serve as silent listeners and as hostesses at Association functions.

Nearly all of the operating budget for the Association has been generated through either State or Federal funding. To date, the Association has had five Hmong Presidents...Vang Lee, Va Xiong, Chue Vang, Thai Lor, and the current President, Lee Kue. The Association working Director is former Laotian military Captain Kue Chaw. There is an additional full time staff of one Caseworker, and one Administrative Assistant. The Association maintains its offices just a few doors down the street from Reverend McKinney and the Garden Creek Baptist Church which has proven so consistently instrumental in building and encouraging the North Carolina Hmong community. Rev. McKinney serves as Secretary to the Board, and for many years has been the key liaison between the Hmong and the surrounding foothills community. The Hmong have generously invited nearby Laotians to become part of the Association, and whenever Laotians are in attendance, the official language of the gatherings switches from Hmong to Laotian.

Since its inception, the Association has been responsible for administering a number of self-help and educational programs. One of them has been the teaching of the English language. This program is both Federally funded and supervised. In addition to many good sides, the program is also fraught with problems. Teachers are not required to speak the Hmong or Laotian languages, and the teaching of Hmong is specifically excluded from funding. To a politician, these restrictions may well seem reasonable. The rationale seems to say: "If the Hmong wish to live in America, they must speak English".

This policy, however good it sounds on paper, is extremely difficult to implement in reality and the success rate is nowhere what it could be if teachers were first required to speak either Hmong or Laotian, and if Hmong students were first given an opportunity to read and write their own language.

Hmong Natural Association Board meeting at the home of Kue Lee.

Wives wait patiently during Board meeting. 19

English teacher Karen Cousins tutors Xee Yang.

The language leap is just too overwhelming for many of the potential students, particularly older Hmong. No common language exists between teacher and student, and more often than not, the student is completely unfamiliar with the learning process being imposed. The North Carolina experience is not unusual. Classes are often undersubscribed, and just in order to keep the program going, the lessons often become private or semi-private tutorials with a "circuit-riding" teacher who visits the Hmong in their homes. In spite of obvious problems, the Hmong, however, are learning. The "tutorial" aspect of the program does provide a measure of courage for otherwise shy persons within a familiar environment.

A second outreach of the Hmong Natural Association has been the collaborative sponsorship, with Warren Wilson College at Swannanoa, of a 30 week "New Roots" program to teach organic vegetable gardening and truck farming. The class was taught by a Warren Wilson instructor and included everything from tailgate marketing…to soil preparation, fertilization, pest and disease control, fruit, flower, and bee culture, greenhouse planting, and a variety of "outside" field trips which visited research programs, and local area producers.

Still another program initiated through the Association has been the formation of the *Hmong New Roots Folk Artists, Incorporated*. This subsidiary of the

20

parent Association comprises some 50 individual Hmong women. The group was formed in 1985 in order to promote markets for Hmong craft, particularly the Hmong flower cloth or "paj ntaub". This subsidiary group has an organizational membership in the Southern Highlands Handicraft Guild, and it regularly exhibits and sells Hmong craft through the several Guild stores and fairs, as well as through other retail outlets. Aside from an Advisory Board of regional arts administrators, the membership of this organization is entirely Hmong.

Other extensions of the Hmong Natural Association have included employment assistance, individual counseling, home visitation, medical transportation, classes in cottage industry sewing techniques, the sponsorship of the annual Hmong New Year festival, and a recently new, innovative pilot program called "Planned Secondary Resettlement".

Kue Chaw, Director, Hmong Natural Association of N.C., Inc.

Association Director Kue Chaw, who earned a degree from Philadelphia's Temple University, was compassionately concerned about the alarming rate of unemployment among the nearly 30,000 Hmong who had regrouped and settled in the San Joaquin Valley of California. Estimates indicate that Hmong unemployment in some areas reached as high as 90%. Communities such as Merced, California, for example, reported that only about 50 of the 4,000 eligible Hmong were employed.

21

Because of the generous California welfare system, many Hmong families were drawing up to 1,000 dollars a month in aid. A few families had the attitude that the U.S. government owed them this support as a debt. Most families, however, wanted to work, but with such generous assistance, it often reached a point where the Hmong felt they would lose money by working...or literally, that they couldn't afford to work for fear of losing welfare benefits.

Director Kue Chaw viewed this situation as a debilitating dilemma, particularly for the traditional Hmong sense of individual worth and dignity. To endlessly sit around, or to gawk at daytime "soaps" in a language they could barely understand...hardly seemed to Kue Chaw to be what the extraordinary human struggle from Laos to the United States had been about. Kue Chaw decided to address this dilemma head on. In a cooperative effort between State and Federal officials, the Hmong Natural Association began the "Planned Secondary Resettlement" program to move some of these welfare recipient, California families to North Carolina.

In order to strive for success, the program needed guidelines. In return for a promise to work in North Carolina and to refrain from welfare, resettled families were to receive 1 month of free rent, a resettlement food allowance of 200 dollars, travel reimbursement from California to North Carolina, a home furnishings allowance (wherein the resettled family could keep the furnishings), and the full support of the Association in dealing with economic, educational, and emotional problems of resettlement. Under Kue Chaw's leadership, North Carolina was the first State to attempt such a program. In the 5 month period between October 1985 and February 1986, seven extended families, or a total of 52 people, were brought from California to North Carolina under this program.

The City of Morganton, North Carolina, particularly its Public Housing Authority, was an important link in the implementation of this program. Morganton renovated many of its public housing units especially for the Hmong. This included fresh paint, new ceilings, new kitchen cupboards, and an overall unit almost as good as new. Nearly all the units involved included 2 floors, 1½ baths, and 3 to 4 bedrooms.

Chao Lor, his wife Mai Ying Lor, and their 3 sons were one of the "Planned Secondary Resettlement" families. Chao's most recent years had involved perpetually pulling up roots. He fled Laos in 1979. As a former member of the Laotian military, he had been employed as a broadcaster on the Laotian radio network. During a year spent in a Thai refugee camp, his life became an exercise in patience and hope.

With the help of a brother-in-law in St. Paul, Chao and his family were finally able to immigrate to Minnesota. Like so many of the Hmong who had been resettled in northern climates, Chao was unprepared for winter. A relative in

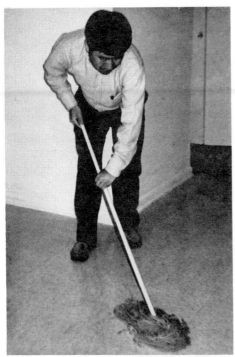

Hmong Association Caseworker Ma Lo prepares a Morganton housing unit for its new Hmong arrivals.

Part of Ma Lo's responsibilities include initially shopping for the arriving family.

Chao Lor, his wife Mai Ying Lor, and their 3 sons arrive from California after a 4 day drive.

(L) Hmong neighbors assist the Lor family with their new couch.

(R) Som Lor helps his parents move in.

Chao Lor and sons Kneb Kou and Som on their first day of school at Hillcrest Elementary School, Morganton, N.C.

Som Lor on his first day of class.

North Carolina invited him for a visit. The visit resulted in nearly one year of residence. Mai Ying was able to find work in a Hickory hosiery mill, even though Chao remained unemployed. He then heard about the "good times" in California, particularly a program to learn English, so the Lor family once again packed up and hit the road. California, however, didn't turn out as expected. Chao spent the next 2 years unemployed in Merced. The language classes were never attended. When his relatives in North Carolina offered him a second opportunity to move back under the new program, he found it an exciting challenge.

The trip from Merced to Morganton was made in 4 days. They encountered snow in both Arizona and New Mexico. Chao drove the family car while a teenage son followed in a second car. Both cars were packed with worldly possessions...a few boxes and bags of clothes, some pots and pans, and a color television set. In California, Chao moved out of a rundown 2 bedroom house. In North Carolina, he moved into a completely renovated Morganton housing unit. Additional funds from the "Planned Secondary Resettlement" program provided him with a new, 3 piece livingroom suite, a dining room set, new beds for all the family members, 200 dollars worth of groceries already stocked in the refrigerator, a month of free rent, a supportive Hmong community anxious to help the Lor family restore its dignity, and the constant caring of the Hmong Natural Association for problems of employment and education.

Rather than offering the short term, California monetary "fix" of welfare, the North Carolina Planned Secondary Resettlement program offered the Lor family an investment in community and in their future. Obviously, the wages in McDowell County are not immediately equal to California welfare payments, but over time, the prognosis for economic stability in North Carolina remains optimistic. As of April, 1986, over one-half of the Hmong in North Carolina had purchased their own homes. Whereas unemployment among the California Hmong had escalated to 90% by 1986, the Hmong unemployment in North Carolina during the same period was less than 5%.

Language, Music, and Musical Instruments
(Special thanks to Dr. Amy Catlin, Ethnomusicologist,
and the Kohler Arts Center, Sheboygan, Wisconsin.)

In order to understand the role of music in the life of the Hmong, it helps to at least temporarily suspend black and white English-American definitions. If you've ever seen a slide show presented with the help of a "dissolve unit", you know that when the projector advances from one slide to another, the images or definitions are mechanically manipulated by the "dissolve" so that one image appears to melt or "dissolve" into another. During this "dissolve", there is a point at which two images overlap...a point at which neither image is securely unique.

Our understanding of the contemporary English word "music" has no equivalent in Hmong. In the life of the Hmong, the idea of "music" being separated from language has no meaning. The two concepts "dissolve" one into the other...they are interwoven...a warp and weft of the same fabric. A fair comparison might be to say that punctuation is to English what music is to Hmong. In other words, if we were to remove punctuation from the English language, we would remove the directional signposts, not to mention embellishment and expressiveness. Likewise, if the Hmong were to remove music from its "dissolve" with language, they would forfeit a similar richness.

Inasmuch as Hmong is a tonal language, it is less concrete, less head-oriented, more amorphous, and definitely more akin to poetry than everyday English. This crossover between language and music manifests itself in nearly all areas of Hmong life...from courtship to politics...and from shamanism to entertainment. Hmong communication...no matter what form it takes...is always therefore vulnerable to some element of abstraction.

Up until recently, scholars believed that the Hmong language belonged to the Sino-Tibetan language family. Today, however, it is believed to be part of a separate language group, along with the *Mien or Yao* group. The Hmong language remained unwritten until early in the 1950's when both French and American missionary linguists, working in Laos, began assigning the language to what is now called the RPA system (Roman Popular Alphabet). This system was used by the missionaries to teach Hmong as a written language.

Although the RPA system remains an acceptable written form for many Laotian Hmong, there are still large numbers of Hmong who have never actually had an opportunity to learn to write their own language. It is therefore not at all unusual to find conflicting spellings, or to find people who communicate a deep sense of embarrassment at not being able to write their own language. It must, however, be clearly pointed out that this confusion in no way reflects upon Hmong language ability. Many of the Laotian Hmong in America have not only learned to read and write English from teachers who cannot speak Hmong, but they are also fluent in Laotian, Thai, and sometimes even French and Chinese.

Hmong words are mostly monosyllabic, beginning with a single consonant or cluster of consonants and then followed by a vowel. Dr. Amy Catlin writes that with both the dialects of Green and White Hmong, there are as many as fifty-seven initial consonants and consonant clusters, each of which can precede any one of fourteen vowels. Dr. Catlin explains that each word is pronounced in one of seven tones, and that each tone variation can also change its meaning. Final consonants do not exist in Hmong.

What all of this means musically is that parallel words take on vastly different meanings, depending upon pitch, whether high, medium, low, rising, falling, breathy, or abrupt. Obviously, there is an unlimited well for nuance in both definition and tonality. Listener participation is therefore an essential part of both linguistic and musical communication.

The Hmong are never very far from some sort of musical connection…be it a cassette player, a musical instrument, or some other form of tonal celebration or lament. Singing often involves improvisation. Poetry is always sung, and varies in subject form from love to struggle, from lament to anecdote, and from history to philosophy. Music is a special part of the Hmong New Year, but it is also an ordinary part of daily life and work. Given their liberty to do so, it would be typical of a Hmong to chant or sing in low tones while performing ordinary chores.

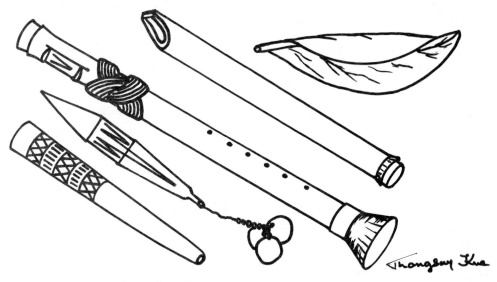

"Ncas", jew's-harp (bottom) with flutes and bamboo leaf whistle.

The "Ncas", Jews-Harp, or Guimbard The "ncas" instrument clearly illustrates the earlier referred to Hmong state of "dissolve" between music and language…where definitions overlap and are neither one, nor the other. The "ncas" is a personal instrument. In its execution, it combines spoken words, verbal tones, and instrumentation all at the same time. The instrument is played by placing the thin, metal blade, or "lemella" of the instrument up against, and between the upper and lower lips, and then plucking the blade to produce vibrations. As the blade resonates, the lips and mouth cavity are manipulated to produce a kind of masked combination of speech and music.

The "ncas" is particularly used in courtship and played by both young men and women. Clever couples can use the instrument as a private form of communication…tones, words, symbols, or fragments combining to form a personal language. The instrument is played by both inhaling and exhaling. The instrument will vary in how it is made…from being crudely fashioned from rough materials on the one hand, to being elegantly embellished (particularly on the case) on the other hand. A lot depends upon the care and the skill of the maker-musician who also, obviously, communicates this skill with presentation.

Shaman Doua Kue illustrates the dance of the "geej".

The "Geej", or Free Reed Mouth Organ Like American symbols of "Uncle Sam", the "Statue of Liberty", or the "Bald Eagle", the "geej" has become the physical symbol for many Laotian-American Hmong. It is an instrument made from six,

29

bamboo, free reed pipes of varying lengths which have been first soaked, steamed and bent into gentle curves. The bamboo pipes are banded together into a cluster, and finally coupled into a wind chamber that holds reserve air, much like the bag on a bagpipe. Actually the instrument has a sound not unlike a bagpipe. The sound is nasal, a kind of drone lament.

According to Dr. Amy Catlin, all six bamboo pipes can resonate at once, but they are never used to produce a single chord. Instead, these pipes are played in patterns of counterpoint to produce intermittent two and three note harmonies connected by melody phrases.

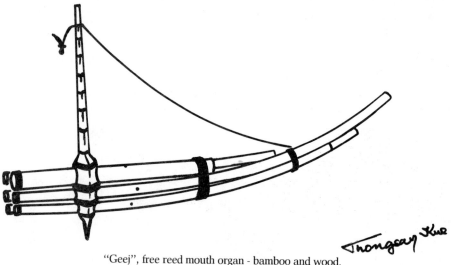

"Geej", free reed mouth organ - bamboo and wood.

The "geej" is traditionally played at the New Year festival while the player executes a complicated series of spins and turns, often in a semi-crouched position, and usually while standing on only one foot at a time. Since the instrument is only played by men, the New Year performance usually means nothing more than a display of skill and masculinity. The same "geej" is, however, also played on other ceremonial occasions such as funerals and weddings where the manner of playing does have special significance. For example, during a Hmong funeral, the "geej" is supposed to be played continuously for three days. During this time, the musician (often a shaman) uses the instrument to directly communicate with the spirit of the deceased, offering direction akin to a "soul path" in order to assist the deceased spirit on its continued journey. This communication with the deceased spirit is ritualized through both the manner in which the instrument is played and also through the sequence of the performer's spins and turns.

30

Many Laotian-American Hmong families own a "geej". It has become an emotional symbol for an earlier life...in its own way, a symbol for the living "soul path" so many Hmong have had to make from Laos, through Thailand, and finally to the United States. If offered a choice in what to bring with from Laos, given the limited space allowance, one of the most prized objects for a Hmong would be the "geej".

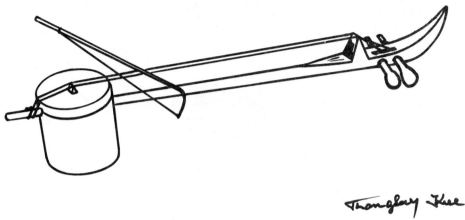

"Tshav Qug", two string violin with bow.

The "Tshav Qug" or Two String Violin This long necked, two string instrument with a drum-like resonating chamber is played with a violin-like bow. The strings are suspended between the resonating drum and the tuning neck. There are no finger frets. The instrument is played as a traditional form of entertainment and is also played during courtship and at the New Year festival.

Flutes and Whistles According to Dr. Amy Catlin, one of the common Hmong flutes is actually a "free reed" bamboo pipe into which a tiny strip of forked metal has been inserted to produce drone-like vibrations similar to the "ncas". Another flute used by the Hmong is much more similar to a recorder or whistle. It produces a sweeter, less buzzing sound.

In Laos, many Hmong were also skilled at producing musical vibrations with the assist of grasses and leaves. These were played in a manner similar to the "ncas". A banana leaf "tshuab nplooj", for example, could be manipulated between the lips and used to produce sound in order to communicate special messages to a girl or boy friend.

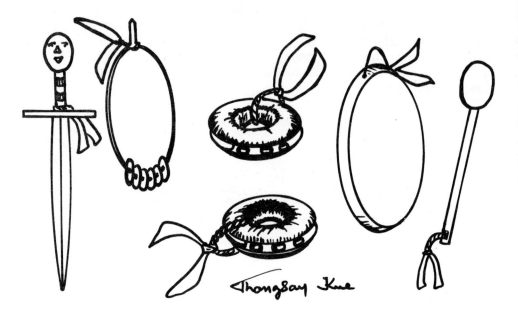

Shaman's percussion instruments - left to right: "ntaaj neeb",
"txiab neeb", "tswb neeb", and "nruas neeb".

Percussion   Several percussion-like instruments are used specifically during either funeral or curing rituals, and these are usually played by a shaman. The "nruas neeb" consists of a circular drum that is resonated with a padded drumstick. The "txiab neeb" or "scissors of the good spirits" is a form of rattle, and the "tswb neeb", usually made out of brass in doughnut form, is a kind of combination bell-rattle. The shaman ritually employs these instruments in either guiding good spirits, or when misleading or admonishing negative spirits.

Contemporary Hmong Rock   It would be inappropriate not to acknowledge the very real and popular presence of electric rock music among "Americanized" Hmong young people. This electronic music employs all the same paraphernalia as does other rock music. It varies in subject from love songs to songs of social commentary. During the annual North Carolina Hmong New Year, electric rock dominates the day. Traditional musicians are allowed a "peep" or two, but the kids claim the day. Once the volume gets turned up, everyone who is either interested or able is out on the dance floor where boogie is king. Tight pants replace pleated skirts, and for at least a few hours of the year, moms and dads loosen the reins while sons with pointed shoes rock with daughters on spike heels.

32

Religion

The Hmong are animistic - they believe, not only in the existence of the soul, but also in the existence of both benevolent and malevolent spirits in nature. It is my understanding that the word "balance" provides a key to understanding a Hmong religious perspective. To a Hmong, the "goal" or "purpose" of life is to maintain *balance*...balance with oneself; with family and friends; one's ancestors; the creatures of earth, sea, and air; forces and manifestations of nature; and with spirits of the unseen world. When humankind, or an individual experiences difficulty or even potential difficulty on this earth...it is usually because some part of the life process is out of *balance*. The point, therefore, within the myriad of Hmong spiritual rituals, is to regain the missing *balance*. When *balance* exists - life continues on course. When *balance* is upset - so too is life upset.

This explanation may well be an oversimplification, but at least it attempts to give a "westerner" some understanding of the Hmong perspective. Too often, we are handed words like "animistic" without any context. These words remain only the jargon for anthropologists until they are offered relevance.

Unlike many religions, the Hmong do not build temples of worship, nor do they acknowledge "graven images". Their homes, and consequently their families, are really the central focus of life. The center post and door of the Hmong house are about the only physical, inanimate objects empowered with anything akin to a "sacred" presence. The Hmong do not have a written or "divine" religious book. Religious life has always centered around oral tradition.

The Hmong believe in a Supreme Being. This Supreme Being resides in the heavens, maintains ultimate power, but remains removed from the everyday, personal ups and downs of each individual. The word "tlan" refers to a spirit. The Hmong believe in the existence of many "tlan". There are "tlan" in the elements of nature, such as a "tlan" of water, and there are "tlan" representing conditions of the human psyche, such as a "tlan" of vengeance. Unlike the Supreme Being, these "tlan" are in touch with everyday, ordinary life on earth, and they are accessible to humans, especially by earthly mediators such as the "txi neng", or Hmong shaman, or by the Hmong exorcist, or oracle.

The Shaman   There are many Hmong "txi neng" (shaman) who have immigrated to the United States. The "txi neng" can be either male or female. This position is not handed down as a blood line inheritance from one generation to another. On the contrary, and as is similar to a "calling" in Christianity, the "txi neng" of the Hmong are "called" into service by supernatural forces.

North Carolina Hmong have two "txi neng". One of them, Doua Kue, has been extremely generous in sharing his home and perspective for this study. Doua lives in a mobile home between Morganton and Marion, North Carolina. He is in

Shaman Doua Kue in his funeral garment.

his early eighties. He serves as "txi neng" for a kin group that is now spread over many parts of the United States. He is therefore occasionally called upon to travel whenever there is need. His function is to cure illness, interpret signs and dreams, predict future events, act as a "broker" between the "tlan" world and the living world, and render security to newborn infants.

Doua Kue's livingroom includes a type of "altar" made from a rectangular wood frame covered over with white and special foil papers. The "altar" includes two shelves or levels which represent the two levels of spiritual life. The lower

34

level is the focus for ritual where earthly interruptions are somewhat minor. The upper level is reserved for the more serious spiritual imbalances. Some of the objects and items contained on the two levels include thin sticks of incense for summoning the spirits, cups filled with uncooked rice in which to hold the incense, hard-boiled eggs, special percussion instruments (as described under the music section) which assist the shaman in summoning and guiding the spirits, additional silver and gold foil paper, candles (which have replaced traditional animal fat lamps), the lower jawbone of a pig, and the two polished halves of a water buffalo horn.

Shaman Doua Kue in front of his "altar".

Across the ceiling and down the opposite wall from Doua Kue's livingroom altar, are two cloth strips about 6 inches wide. These are accompanied by two fine threads. The strips and threads represent a bridge between the two levels of the spiritual world. Shaman Kue tries to remain under the protection of these cloth strips and threads when performing rituals.

The lower pig jawbone which the shaman uses during ritual is dedicated to healing. Its powers come from the "tlan" and are secured through a special, ritual sacrifice of the pig. The jawbone is used only one year, and then burned so that the spirit of the pig can be reborn. The lower jawbone of a cow, water buffalo, or chicken can also, by special ritual, contain similar powers. The two halves of shaman Kue's water buffalo horn have also been dedicated to healing, and selected in a manner similar to that for the pig. The two halves of horn are used as omens, or in a sense, as a way to "diagnose" an illness. Shaman Kue rattles and clicks the horns in one hand and then literally throws them onto a flat surface in order to take a "reading". The throw is not unlike the "throw" involved in the familiar I Ching.

As previously mentioned, the Hmong believe that illness results from a condition of spiritual imbalance. They believe that at various times during the life cycle, the soul either tries to leave the body, or falls into a state of disrepair. The throw of the water buffalo horns gives the shaman a "reading" as to both the nature of the illness and an insight into the outcome. A symbolic burning of paper foil is also involved in this ritual. Paper foil symbolizes money. A throw resulting in two open horn halves can mean that the soul will immediately return, that no serious illness or interruption of the spirit is involved, and that the ritual burning of foil has been accepted. A throw of one horn half up, and one horn half down indicates that the spirit will return to the body. A throw resulting in the two horn halves facing down can either mean that the soul is not allowed to return to the body, or that more foil must be burned, or that a rethrow is necessary.

Perhaps it would be helpful to describe the Hmong religious perspective as something one *lives*, rather than as something one *professes*. Spiritual awareness traditionally permeates all areas of Hmong life - no part left untouched. Many rituals are performed exclusively by the shaman, but a myriad of rituals and acknowledgements also require direct participation by each individual. These rituals range in scope from exorcism, to rituals directed at changing one's fortune or direction, to rituals recalling lost spirits, to rituals associated with illness, death, and the afterlife, and to almost routine, daily rituals which simply acknowledge elements in the natural world. Our space here does not allow detailed descriptions of all Hmong rituals. Sufficient to say that we intend only to provide a sense of the religious overview. We apologize for the brevity of this survey, and hope that this rich subject can be expanded upon in future volumes.

Christianity   Our Laotian-American Hmong, for the most part, have diligently tried to support Christianity. They've joined Christian churches all across America. Sunday after Sunday, they bow their heads in Christian prayer, repeat our hymns and responsive readings, and dutifully try to understand our Judeo-Christian traditions. Often, and in spite of tremendous effort, they still haven't the foggiest idea what's going on. Oh yes, they can certainly *see* and *hear* what's going on. That's obvious! But from a gut level, they still can't *feel* what's going on.

Our religion is not theirs! The pressures to change are upon the Hmong - not upon Christians. In a brief condensation of earthly time, the Hmong are asking themselves to complete a giant leap of history and culture. It is not easy to support the world of "tlan" in contemporary America. It is not easy to live in a land of doctors, medicines, and hospitals, and still find room for the "txi neng". And even the "txi neng" himself is caught between two worlds as he waits in the reception room of his American doctor for a prescription to alleviate the pain of his headache.

The "tlan" world is fading. It is caught between 4,000 years of history and a contemporary American world of concrete and Christ. Today's Laotian-American Hmong are the generation in transition. They have had to confront enormous grief. They have had to confront the loss of a world they left behind. Sometimes their confusion is still very real. Sometimes the ache, the loneliness, and the emptiness won't go away.

But our Hmong are trying. Sometimes they try harder than we can ever imagine. Americans have had several generations to get used to themselves. The Hmong are just beginning to get used to themselves in our image. They don't need our sympathy. They do need our welcome!

Clothing

English language publications usually refer to traditional Hmong garments as "costume". For our purposes, it seems more accurate to use the word "clothing". We do not subscribe to the notion that everyday garments are "costume". In America, the word "costume" has too often come to mean items of apparel that are used to "dress up in", as in "Halloween", or "Mardi Gras" costume. Traditional Hmong garments are as ordinary to tens of thousands of Hmong, as tee-shirts are common to Americans.

Traditional Hmong styles are, however, being rapidly infiltrated and re-placed by "western" style. This is almost as true in southeast Asia as in America. These changes are really not much different than the changes affecting the garments of ethnic minorities all over the world. How much of the change is directly attributable to hard-sell "western" advertising still needs to be deter-mined. What we do know, however, is that male-female contrasts, even within the same family, are abrupt and obvious. Whereas women tend to caretake ethnic tradition and identity, men tend to emulate a new identity which manifests itself somewhere between the "Marlboro Man", on the one hand, and the "discount" store version of the small town banker, on the other hand. This male-female "push-pull" is clearly visible within the Laotian-American Hmong family. Whereas Hmong women still thoughtfully caretake ethnic clothing, their men tend to abandon traditional clothing altogether. Nowhere is this more evident in America than at the annual Hmong New Year festival where it is all too common a sight to see a Hmong father wearing a "western" business suit, while a mother and her daughters continue to celebrate traditional clothing. Why men are so quick to change into American camouflage is the purview of the cultural anthropologist. If cultural intimidation is one of the ingredient pressures for change, then it seems fair to say that Hmong women must be less vulnerable to intimidation than men.

The John Michael Kohler Arts Center, P.O. Box 489, Sheboygan, Wisconsin, 53082, has published a comprehensive study on Hmong ethnic clothing which we recommend. The publication is authored by Joanne Cubbs, and is entitled: *Hmong Art: Tradition and Change*. The Chinese publication *Clothings and Ornaments of China's Miao People* is another excellent resource book on Hmong clothing.

Kinship through clothing, or in other words, garments which establish a Hmong ethnic identity, have become the exclusive responsibility of women. Hmong men do not traditionally sew or weave. They often help in the process of growing, harvesting, or preparing fiber, but they do not usually translate fiber into fabric or garments. In Laos, needlework and textile skills are passed from mother to daughter in companionship and caring. Little girls begin to mimic and learn adult skills as soon as they are able to coordinate their finger movements. As with many cultures, how well a woman performs with fiber is a clear measure of her status, her eligibility as a marriage partner, and her potential contribution to family and kin group. Being sloppy or disinterested has no reward. A wise mother makes it very clear to her daughter that excellence in textile skills must never be compromised.

Hmong women are consequently renowned and respected for their meticulous textile craftsmanship. Their excellence and authority not only extends to plant cultivation, but it also extends to knowing how to transform the plant into fibers, as well as how to spin, weave, dye, and stitch the fiber. In applying her skills, she has also consequently become a reservoir for preserving and transcribing Hmong symbols, patterns, and folk stories. She and the Hmong shaman are the "keepers" of the Hmong culture. The fibers used in Hmong textiles, depending upon geographical location, vary from cotton, to linen, to wool, to felt, and finally to hemp.

(L) Book illustrator Thongsay Kue poses wearing traditional clothing.

(R) Detail, Thongsay Kue's headdress made by his mother. 39

As in many cultures, Hmong garments vary according to their use. Some clothes are less special and are used for daily work, while others are reserved for family celebrations such as weddings, births, courtships, funerals, or for the annual Hmong New Year festival. In connection with clothing, the Hmong New Year symbolizes continuance through harvest…taking on a new skin while shedding the old…exchanging old garments for new.

Men's Clothing   Traditional Laotian Hmong male apparel makes use of black. The black pants resemble two identical, equilateral triangles sewn together with openings left at the three points. One opening is for the waist, while the other two are for the legs. The garment is worn with one point of the two sewn triangles as if hanging from the waist, but yet attached at the ankles by the other two outside triangle points. The garment has no crotch. The bottom line of the triangle just sort of hangs "loose", and moves into folds of cloth as the legs are moved. It's a very comfortable garment to wear.

Director Kue Chaw and his wife Mao Moua in traditional clothing.

The Hmong male also wears a shirt or blouse, usually white, and depending upon how hot or cold it is, this can be covered with either a vest or a black, long sleeved jacket. When dressing for special occasions, the man also wears a sash, a jewelry breast plate suspended from around the neck, a belt decorated with coins, sandals, shoulder bag, and a headdress which can vary from a simple skull cap to an elaborate reverse applique explosion of color festooned with tiny pompoms.

Women's Clothing   Around the house, in an atmosphere of privacy, Hmong women often wear a blouse tucked into a type of sarong. When out in public, however, they can often boggle the eyes with incredible displays of textile handskills and color, not to mention a sense of undisputed presence within the person. To put it mildly, when a Hmong woman gets "dressed to the hilt", some of the rest of us might feel like a poor excuse for Seventh Avenue.

For special occasions, it takes her about 20 minutes to dress. After her undergarments, she begins by wrapping her calves, between the knees and ankles, with black triangles of cloth that form into leggings. Some say the leggings were a protection from insects and scratches...others say it was somewhere between modesty and a deliberate effort to exaggerate the calf girth in order that it appear more attractive. After the leggings comes a blouse and then a jacket that has a sailor-like, embroidered collar which hangs down the back.

Traditionally, the pleated, batik-dyed and heavily embroidered, appliqued skirt was the signature of Hmong womanhood. In former times Hmong women were known to wear as many as 20 skirts over one another at the same time. The bottom tier on an average skirt contains about 6½ yards of fabric. It is like a giant textile accordian wrapped around the waist. It undulates, and has a presence unto itself when worn.

Many stories surround the origin of the pleated skirt. One folk tale attributes the pleats from the Chinese "Golden Pheasant", while another tale suggests origins from the underside dome pleats on many forest mushrooms. A medium-sized pleated skirt contains some 325 separate pleats. A large-sized skirt can contain as many as 500 individual pleats. Some say the pleats used to be folded into half an appropriate length of bamboo. Small holes were poked into the bamboo, and then the second half of the bamboo was placed over the folded pleats as a cover. This closed length was then held over steam in order to permanently crease the pleats.

Each time a pleated Hmong skirt is worn, the wearer removes up to 16 horizontal gathering threads (spaced from waist to hem) that help maintain the permanence of the pleats. Once the wearer has completed wearing the skirt, these horizontal gathering threads are carefully restitched through each pleat and then left in place during storage. The gathering threads are pulled tight to

41

secure the pleats. At this point, the pleats are so tightly gathered together that the skirt resembles thick cardboard. It is stored in this stiff condition. Since each pleat is a fold representing two thicknesses of material, a single needle and thread must therefore pass through over 10,000 thicknesses of material each time a medium-sized Hmong skirt is worn and then put away. What a very different sense of caretaking this represents than the "western" teenage girl who dumps her skirt into a heap on the floor of her bedroom!

Hmong folklore is rich with stories about patterns, and designs, especially in regard to pleated skirts. One story tells of a clever young girl who stitched a snakeskin pattern onto the hem of her skirt for protection. She did so, because she realized that snakes rarely attack each other. Another story tells of an old Hmong grandmother who stitched a flag pattern onto her jacket and skirt in the hope of locating a long, lost son who had been taken away and conscripted into a foreign army. The two eventually got together when the son recognized his special flag.

Still another story tells about two brothers migrating away from their former village because of continual war. Just as they were about to leave, the younger brother stopped along the road and decided to paint village sights onto his clothing as a way to remember his former life. Squares were supposed to represent land, red stripes meaning fish, curved lines meaning mussels and stars, wavy lines meaning trees, and thick stripes as representations of major rivers. In a similar folktale, symbols were supposed to be a kind of language. This story dates back to early China when Chinese authorities were supposed to have prohibited the Hmong from speaking their own language. The story tells how the women devised symbols of communication and then stitched these symbols onto their skirts…often poking fun at their oppressors. One final story of origin tells of a very old Hmong tradition to add a band of green to the hem of a 3-tiered skirt upon the birth of a first child.

After the skirt, the next addition to clothing for special occasions is the breastplate pendant, and other jewelry. Next is the black waist wrap. It is usually about 8 inches wide by about 7 yards long. It is doubled in half, wrapped, and then followed by a narrow, front apron panel, and then a belt decorated with coins, or if one doesn't have such a belt, then by a wide sash wrapped twice around the waist and tied at the back. The extraordinary Hmong "turban" or headwrap is the final "crown" to women's traditional apparel. This is a strip of cloth (maroon for White Hmong) which is about 12-14 inches wide and in length of up to 9 yards. It is wrapped time after time around the head and finally held in place by strips of decorated ribbon that cross in an "X" at the center of the forehead. When the headwrap is properly tied, it can add two inches to a woman's height. Hmong women also occasionally carry a shoulder bag, but it is more common for them to tuck valuables inside their waist sash. Sometimes in north

42

(text continued on page 56)

1. Silver breastplate and head ornament, Guizhou province, China. Silver symbolizes light dispelling evil. *Courtesy: Clothings and Ornaments of China's Miao People*, Nationality Press, 1985, Beijing.

43

2. Batik and cross stitch pleated skirt and jacket, Nandan county, Yueli area, China. *Courtesy: Clothings and Ornaments of China's Miao People*, Nationality Press, 1985, Beijing.

3. "Horn" hairstyle of false hair twisted around a long comb, Agong, Zhijin, China. *Courtesy: Clothings and Ornaments of China's Miao People*, Nationality Press, 1985, Beijing.

4. Pleated skirt and jacket, Luobo river area, Guizhou, China. *Courtesy: Clothings and Ornaments of China's Miao People*, Nationality Press, 1985, Beijing.

5. Reverse applique baby carrier by Ma Thao, Courtesy - John Michael Kohler Arts Center.   47

48   6. Detail, reverse applique "flower cloth" by Chia Lee Xiong, Courtesy - John Michael Kohler Arts Center.

7. Flight to Thailand, "flower cloth" detail, Courtesy - Hmong Natural Association.

49

8. Corn Grinding, "flower cloth" detail, Courtesy - Hmong Natural Association.

9. In the fields, Thailand, "flower cloth" detail, Courtesy - Hmong Natural Association.

10. Bamboo and thatch, "flower cloth" detail, Courtesy - Hmong Natural Association.

11. "Flower cloth" detail, Courtesy - Hmong Natural Association.   51

52   12. Hmong child, northern Thailand.

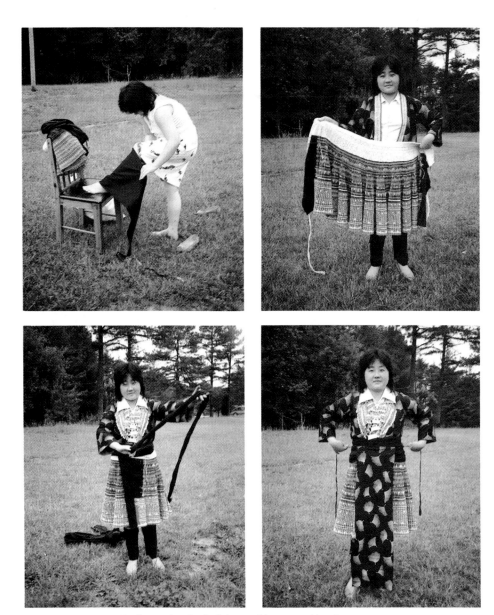

13. (Top L) Maytong Kue begins her festival dress with wrapped leggings.
14. (Top R) Maytong's skirt contains 325 separate pleats.
15. (Bottom L) Maytong puts on her aluminum breastplate pendant and begins the 7 yards of waist wrap.
16. (Bottom R) Front apron.

53

17. (Top L) Waist sash wrapped twice, tied at the back.
18. (Top R) Maytong begins to wrap the 9 yards of dark maroon for her turban-like headwrap.
19. (Bottom L) Complete festival dress, back view.
20. (Bottom R) Complete festival dress, Maytong Kue.

54

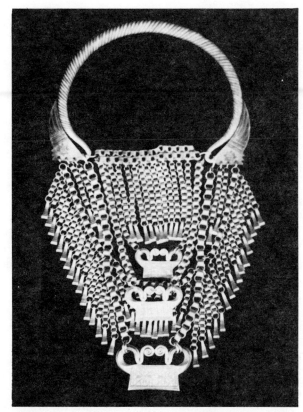

(Above) Silver pendant breastplate belonging to Mao Moua.
(Below) Silver earrings and bracelet belonging to Mao Moua.

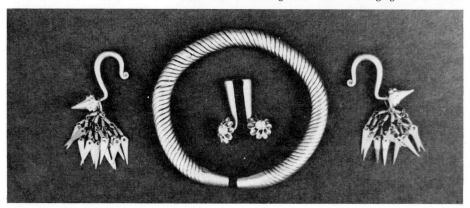

55

Thailand I have seen Hmong women with so much tucked into their waist sashes that they looked as though they had distended tummies.

Hmong Jewelry As with many cultures, jewelry, particularly silver jewelry, is akin to a system of investment or banking. Women are traditionally the keepers and protectors of this investment. During periods of affluence, jewelry is heavy silver. Today, however, during times of Hmong resettlement, many refugee women have had to sell their silver, and replace traditional breastplate pendants with aluminum reproductions. The breastplate pendant design which appears with the "geej" on the signboard of the Hmong Natural Association of North Carolina is a symbol of peace.

Hmong Colors For the most part, what Americans see as Hmong color is an "educated" color sense. This "educated" color owes its origin to "western" relief workers within Thai refugee camps. Our understanding is that some of the early workers saw Hmong refugee women applying their extraordinary needlework skills on colors which the workers felt to be unmarketable to a "western" audience. Refugees needed money, workers tried to be "instructive" in color-marketing, and colors consequently changed. What we now see coming from Thailand, and from many parts of the United States, are colors with a consistent, subtle and sophisticated tonal quality. These are not traditional Hmong colors. The Hmong love glitz, as well as dayglow-like pinks, greens, and magentas. They love an explosion of color, rather than controlled tonal subtlety. If left to their own choice, Laotian-American Hmong women tend to gravitate to bright chemical dyes over vegetable dyes, and they tend to prefer synthetics (because of their price, sheen, and availability) over natural fibers.

The "Paj Ntaub" Flower, or Story Cloth Our guess, although unconfirmed by other research, is that the squares and rectangles of reverse applique and cross-stitch embroidery which Americans have now become familiar with as products of the Hmong, are not really traditional to the Hmong culture. We believe these varying squares and rectangles to be another off-shoot and by-product of "western" marketing within the Thai refugee camps. This does not, however, diminish their value, or their excellence in craftsmanship. It's just that we are unaware of large "wall-hanging" textiles as a traditional part of the Hmong culture.

We believe that what actually happened is that with time on their hands, extraordinary skill, and with guidance from relief workers...Hmong women began to cut, fold, and stitch what has now become a new Hmong "art" form. Many of these so-called "paj ntaub" textiles celebrate traditional Hmong symbols for elements in nature. Others tell stories, often tiger stories, exodus stories, or depict Hmong folkways through embroidery, such as cock fights, or traditional ways of grinding corn.

For those of us who have been lucky enough to visit the Hmong in southeast Asia, we have seen their "old" work. The scale of the former reverse applique is so tiny that it often seems impossible to believe that human hands could have cut, folded, and stitched the materials in place. It is even more remarkable when one realizes that human fingers have additionally achieved spiraling designs with these same techniques. The original colors on these "old" textiles are gay...rarely subtle. It is therefore our somewhat "educated guess" that "paj ntaub" in its original connotation was meant to identify a kind of joyful, needlework surface embellishment on garments, baby carriers, and other household textile objects. We do not believe it was intended to be loaned out as a term to include giant contemporary wall hangings, tablecloths, pillowcases, bookmarks, and the other myriad of commercial items now available in America. "Paj ntaub" is now used as a "catch-all" phrase to describe nearly everything produced in textiles by Hmong women. We cannot hope to stop the new use of the word, but we can at least take a responsibility to underline its original intent.

The Green (Blue) Hmong Loom   The traditional Green (Blue) Hmong loom is a combination backstrap-vertical frame loom. It is much more sophisticated than the typical backstrap loom where warp threads are simply tied around a convenient upright. The Hmong loom incorporates a castle-like structure which, in this particular instance, is a long rectangular frame tied at an angle to a wall with its heddle control, back warp beam, and shed control bar suspended from the castle-like structure. The warp tension is achieved by a backstrap which is tied to a cloth beam in front of the weaver's waist. The weaver's foot is looped with a string and tied to a heddle bar so that when the string is pulled, the heddle bar is depressed.

Hemp Into Cloth   The hemp plant is common to most areas of southeast Asia, and the Hmong have traditionally used hemp fibers to produce fabric for garments. The fiber is heavier than cotton, but similar to linen, except that when it's woven, it seems looser, and not as "hard" as linen. Hemp fiber actually feels like what we refer to as "homespun". The process of converting the hemp plant into fiber is similar to the process of retting flax into linen. It involves breaking down the woody tissue of the stalk, separating fibers from this tissue, and then softening the fibers in preparation for spinning. Stalks are dried in the sun, broken in half, and then the fibers are peeled away from the stalks. They are then softened by pounding them with a wooden mallet in a shallow earth depression. This process also helps remove residue stalk still clinging to the fibers. The fibers are then stored until they are spun into thread for weaving.

Some of the other processes used in preparing hemp include bleaching the   57

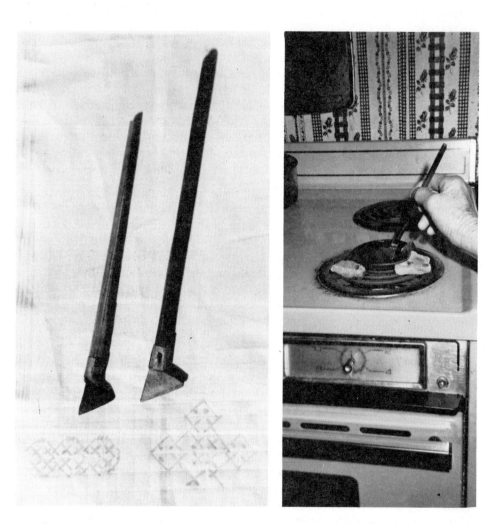

(L) Wax reservoir tools used for batik.

(R) Wax is slowly and carefully heated over electric burner.

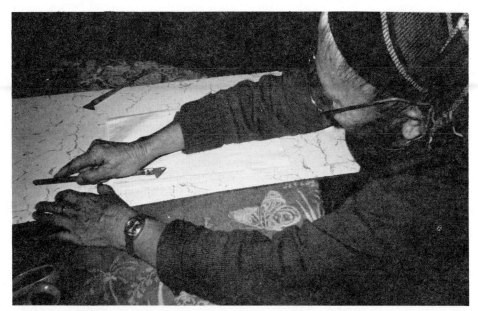

Ying Lee freehands hot wax batik designs on fabric before dyeing.

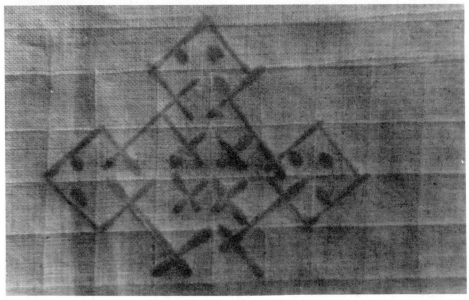

Detail, wax design on fabric before dyeing.

thread in a bath of woodash, sizing it in a solution containing beeswax, and finally flattening the thread before it is warped.

Wax Resist Batik, or "Cab Daaj Tab" Along with cross stitch and reverse applique, Hmong textiles are recognized by their batik designs. These designs are traditional, and are passed from mother to daughter. They are drawn freehand from memory onto the fabric. In Laos, the Hmong used beeswax as a resist. A tool called a "dlav ua tab cab" was used for drawing. It was usually handmade and contained a wooden handle and a small triangular copper wax reservoir with a hole in the bottom. Some women were so familiar with resist drawing, they used only their eyes as a guide. Other women would first crease portions of the design (at least the straight lines) into the fabric by turning the fabric at the design line, and then creasing a fold line that could later be followed with the resist reservoir tool. The process is to draw a design onto the fabric with hot wax, dye the fabric in cold water with a sequence of dye baths (depending on the desired density of color), and finally rinsing the batiked and dyed fabric in hot water to remove the wax.

We have invested considerable energy to find out the name of the Laotian plant which is used to produce the deep blue (indigo blue) color. Previously published reports vary from claims of berries on the one hand, to a plant called "Iresine Herbsti" or Beefsteak on the other hand. None of the descriptions given by North Carolina Hmong fit either of these two sources. What we do know is that the plant is about 36 inches high, has a finger-shaped blue flower, has a wheat-like stalk, and also has medicinal uses as a poultice for fever, especially malaria.

We are told that the plant stalk is cut, and then soaked for at least 3 days, or until the leaves and stalk fibers begin to break down. It is then gathered up, squeezed, and removed from the bath. The bath soaking solution is then strained through cloth in order to remove all bits and pieces of residue fiber. This solution is then re-heated, woodash is added as both a color intensifier and fixative, and then the fabric is added to the solution. The Hmong believe that pregnant women should not come in contact with either the dye solution or the dyeing process. They believe contact increases the risk of stillborn children.

Hmong Customs

Families and Names In Laos, before the refugee exodus, there were some 12 separate Hmong family kin groups which were distinguishable by separate family names. The importance of kinship, particularly kinship in good standing, is clearly reviewed by author Timothy Dunnigan in the 1986 Kohler Arts Center publication entitled *Hmong Art, Tradition and Change*. Dunnigan writes that: "Anyone who is inconstant in kinship loyalty can be compared to a 'dog without a

60

master'. Such an animal wanders from one campfire to the next, living on scraps. Unless a person permanently joins a Hmong kin group and contributes to the common good, he or she will not receive the support necessary in times of crisis when others must make sacrifices on their behalf". Dunnigan retells a Hmong tale which says: "A Hmong who tries to gain membership in another kin group is called a 'puav' or bat. Such a creature tries in vain to convince the birds that he is one of them because he has wings and can fly. The bat is rejected for having the nose of a mouse and furry skin. When the bat goes to the mice, he is rebuffed for being too much like a bird. Hmong are consequently very skeptical about the possibility of ever being fully accepted within other kin groups".

All Hmong carry their family or kin group name. In Laos, there used to be clear traditions with regard to names and naming. For example, in Laos, and at birth, a male child was traditionally given his family name plus a personal name which often embodied hope or protection for the growing child. Such a male child would have been known by his family name first, followed by a personal name second. To illustrate this example, the Director of the North Carolina Hmong Natural Association goes by the name Kue Chaw. *Kue* is his family name, and *Chaw* (meaning blanket or bridge) is his second or personal name. In this way, Laotian Hmong could immediately identify a person's family. Later, upon reaching manhood, marriage, or upon the birth of a first child, the individual was traditionally given a second personal name. The selection of this second personal name was usually agreed upon by the bride's parents in cooperation with the groom's parents. In the example of Director Kue Chaw, he was additionally given the name *Chu* upon the birth of his first child (*Chu* meaning owner). This second personal name usually came last in order.

Upon arriving in the United States, many Hmong tried to adopt American ways by re-arranging names with their family or kin name last, and their personal name first. This often causes confusion to a westerner who knows a Hmong by a personal name first, but hears other Hmong address the same person using the family name first. Even within the Hmong community, some individuals have retained the order of their names, while others have opted for re-arrangement.

Female Hmong children usually identify themselves by their personal names, but after marriage, they take on the family or kin name of their husband. Sometimes family names indicate certain food taboos. For example, the *Kue* family name is allowed to eat all foods whereas the *Yang* family is supposed to avoid eating heart in all animals, fish, and fowl. Another taboo is that individuals with the same family name should avoid inter-marriage.

Courtship Specifics of courtship are mentioned in several other areas of the text, such as the role the "ncas" or jewharp plays in developing an intimate

61

"Pav pob" New Year courtship game involving ball toss and poetry.

courtship language, or the importance of the Hmong New Year Festival as a forum for advertising availability. During this annual festival, young people of marriageable age play a game called "pav pob" where a line of young men face a line of young women. Small balls are then tossed back and forth between lines while a form of courtship poetry is exchanged. In theory, the game is played to demonstrate wit and ability. In practice, it provides an opportunity for teasing, flirting, and getting to know the opposite sex.

We asked several men in the Hmong community to describe desireable characteristics in a potential wife. The most important consideration was always *family*. Is the girl from a good family? Does her family work hard, and are the family relationships loyal? In many ways, the Hmong look upon a marriage of individuals as also a marriage of families.

The second priority in a mate are domestic skills. Can she cook, garden, raise animals, keep a house, and is she a courteous hostess? Thirdly, the men listed energy level as a desireable characteristic. Is the girl a hard worker, or is she lazy? Finally came physical appearance, but this didn't seem to be as important as other priorities. The men we questioned had all reached physical maturity in Laos. We would expect very different priorities from young men reaching maturity within the United States...or, at least a different order of priority. We expect that many of the young Hmong men in North Carolina are seriously thinking about marriage outside the Hmong community. Supposedly the values expressed by men in mate selection are similar to the values of women.

Young men and women are allowed to actively participate in the mate selection process, but they undoubtedly receive substantial input and pressure (advice?) from their families. Once selection is made, family negotiations soon take place. Each family selects one or two neutral individuals who negotiate, or in a sense "broker" the details of the agreement. The use of a neutral go-between circumvents direct family-to-family confrontation.

Marriage negotiations usually focus on the matter of "bride price", or in other words, what sort of gifts the groom and his family are prepared to offer the family of the bride. In Laos, this often centers around the numbers of livestock to be offered, such as how many chickens or cows. Many Hmong women feel that the "bride price" later becomes a husband's wedge of control by continuously reminding his wife about how much she cost him in "bride price". In Laos, courtship for girls begins around age 14. Most men prefer virgin brides. Women seldom have the luxury of the same expectations inasmuch as men are allowed more than one wife. Even though most Hmong women go along with this tradition, they are quick to point out that multiple wives divide a man's heart. In Laos, it is not uncommon for couples to elope. We are told that it would be quite typical for a boy to show up at the home of his girl friend and ask her to run off with him. According to tradition, she must refuse. "No, no", she will say. "Yes, yes", he will reply. "No, no", she again says, but off they go. This verbal refusal (even though she leaves) is to protect herself in the event of an unhappy marriage where she can later claim that she refused. Even when couples elope, the family-to-family negotiations still take place surrounding "bride price".

Marriage Traditional Hmong marriage is embellished by elaborate preparation, symbolic ceremony, and extensive feasting. Depending upon the economic affluence of the families involved, the wedding can last anywhere from one to three days. Gift exchange between the two families, as well as elaborate food preparation will always precede the wedding. On the actual day of the wedding, guests gather around midday. The ceremony consists of basically three parts. During the first part, spokesmen selected by each of the families compete in a kind of verbal "give and take" involving admonishments to both families about courtesy in their future relationships with one another. During the second part of the ceremony, the groom addresses each individual family member of the bride and expresses his verbal appreciation for permission to marry his bride. During the final part, the groom introduces his bride to his ancestors.

A Hmong wedding does not contain Christian-like vows. The actual marriage ritual involves tying a length of white ribbon or string from around the wrist of the bride to around the wrist of the groom. This tying is performed by a respected elder or pair of elders who accompany themselves with chants. A young hen, rooster, and an egg are also a part of the ceremony as symbols for the coming together of all parts. Candles and burning incense alert the spirit world to the fact that a marriage is taking place and should be noted. After the hard-boiled egg has been halved, each marriage partner eats one of the halves.

63

Extensive toasting then takes place, and the groom is supposed to acknowledge each toast, while at the same time trying to remain sober. When the feasting finally takes place, the bride and groom sit separately. There is no rush to finish eating. It can go on for hours, and provides a further opportunity for families to get to know each other.

After marriage, a woman must not only prove that she is able to carry out her household responsibilities, but she is also supposed to prove her modesty and loyalty. According to tradition, and during the first year of marriage, she is not supposed to make eye contact, or conversation with other men, nor should she smile at other men. During her first year, her male contacts are supposed to remain formal.

Menstruation, Pregnancy, and Childbirth   When a Hmong woman is pregnant, she continues her normal routine of diet and work. One old adage warns that a pregnant woman should not reach above her head for fear of "loosening" the baby. There is also an old adage about the blood from both childbirth and menstruation. Blood must not be left exposed to negative spirits for fear of sickness or pain as resulting retribution. The textiles or cloths used to absorb blood during childbirth and menstruation are supposed to be carefully washed in a basin (never in a river). The water must then be buried in a hole where the blood can return to the earth. If blood should reach a stream or river, it is believed there will be punishment. The Hmong feel that spirits may cause a woman to miss her period, or to experience heavy menstrual cramps. They also believe that eating or drinking cold food during menstruation may cause the blood to clot, and may cause cramps.

It is common for a husband to attend the birth of his children, and also to participate in tying off the umbilical cord. After birth, a woman is not supposed to leave her house for 30 days. She builds back her strength with a steady diet of boiled chicken and rice, and while nursing, she should try to avoid eating onions and cucumber. Onions are believed to cause a form of gas or colic, while cucumbers encourage diarrhea.

Divorce   Divorce is permitted within the Hmong culture, but not before extensive efforts have been made within the community to sort out the marriage problems. This is done, not only to define the real reasons for conflict, but also to determine if avenues still remain open for reuniting the couple. It appears to be less difficult for a man to seek divorce than for a woman. If a divorce is agreed upon, the male children often remain with the father, while the female children remain with the mother. During negotiations, there will be attention focused on whether or not the woman was a "willing" bride, or whether she was pressured by her parents. If divorce is approved, it is not unusual for the bride to forfeit her "bride price". If a woman simply leaves a marriage without divorce, she risks losing all of her children in addition to forfeiting her "bride price". Once divorce has been finally approved, there is apparently no negative stigma attached to the divorced person.

A Few Additional Customs   In Hmong, birth placenta is referred to as the "shirt". If a child is a male, the placenta used to be traditionally placed on either side of the central house post as a symbol of male responsibility and family lineage. If the child was female, the placenta was placed at one of the house corners, a symbol that the female will one day leave the family and join the kin group of her husband. Placenta was also an important consideration during funeral rites. Those who gathered in order to assist the departed spirit on its forward journey in the afterlife, prayed that the "shirt" or placenta would rejoin the departed spirit to help sustain it during the journey.

-Traditionally, in Laos, men used to shave all the hair off the front of the head...leaving a long, braided and coiled topknot at the back of the head. The long "tail" was thought to embody the spirit of the male. It was therefore groomed and preserved. In Laos, men also traditionally wore beards, even though few Hmong continue this custom in America.

-In Laos, men were allowed to have more than one wife. Usually, having more than one wife indicated either a position of wealth or power. Many of the Hmong who immigrated to the United States brought more than one wife. These second wives were identified as either sisters or sisters-in-law if immigration authorities ever bothered to ask.

-In families with children from more than one adult female, all children are treated with equal respect. The children do not place much significance on either half or full blood connections. Half and full brothers and sisters are just all part of the same family.

-Inasmuch as Hmong families are patriarchal, men traditionally make most of the major family decisions. A wise male will, however, carefully hear out a wife's opinions. Within family life, the women generally serve the men. If there are several males within a household, the men eat ahead of the women, and they eat together. Families are usually large, and divisions within a household are frowned upon. It would be much more traditionally Hmong for household members to act in unison than to act as individuals. Within a Hmong family, advancing age is given maximum respect. The Hmong care for their own - diligently.

-After having a child, a new mother is not supposed to go outside for at least one month. She is also admonished not to eat salty food or drink cold water.

-Men are not allowed to have sex with their brother's wives. This taboo covers

65

divorced couples, but excludes situations where there is a death. The Hmong used to believe that breaking this taboo could result in blindness.

-In public places, a wife is supposed to stand to the left of her husband. Female children stand to the left of their mother and male children to the right of their father.

-In Laos, if you were visited by a Hmong leader, it was customary to show respect in public by always walking on the left side of the leader, and slightly (about ½ step) behind.

Bark-cut boundary marker used in the forests of northern Laos.

Woven bamboo warning sign placed in front of door to notify visitors not to enter and that shaman has visited in order to cure an illness.

Traditional Structures

Houses Hmong domestic architecture will vary according to the availability of local building material, extremes in seasonal temperature, and according to the amount of rainfall. Houses located in lower elevations, such as in the hotter regions of Thailand and Vietnam, are built for tropical and semi-tropical lifestyles. These houses are often elevated off the ground, anywhere from 3 to 8 feet. They are accessible by either log steps or bamboo ladders, and they are built upon stout posts or "stilts". Elevating the structures takes full advantage of breeze, insures maximum dryness above damp earth, minimizes human contact with insects, rodents, and snakes, and provides a shaded and dry work and storage space underneath the house. The traditional tool the Hmong use to dig holes for house posts is called a "toom txhob".

Hmong house, north Laos, bark-strip roof.

The skeleton of one of these houses is traditionally built by lashing together ribs of bamboo. Interior and exterior walls are made by weaving green bamboo which has been soaked and split. Alternative wall materials can be local grasses and reeds, or even bundles of rice straw stacked to cover openings or to make partitions. In hot areas, walls are often woven as detachable panels that can be either tilted out, or completely lifted out to allow for air circulation. In more temperate climates, woven walls tend to be more permanent, rigid, and dense.

The most common weaving pattern resembles our "Herring Bone", or "Twill". Other variations include "Diamond Twill", and "Plain Weave", with either single or double staves. In lower elevations and for field shelters, the roofing material is either rice straw thatch, or large skewered leaves applied as shingles.

68

Traditional thatching in Thailand and parts of Laos consists of constructing individual thatch shingles and then layering these shingles in rows, one over the other, beginning at the eaves and working toward the peak. A shingle is made by first cutting a thin stave of bamboo about one-half inch wide by two to three feet long. Rice straw is then folded over the stave, evenly spread out along the stave to a desired thickness, and then sewn tightly to the stave, just below the fold, with a stitch similar to what westerners call "Soumak". For the most part, synthetic cord, which resists rot, has now replaced traditional sewing materials.

Laotian thatch tends to be thicker and more matted than Thai thatch. The threat of fire has turned many Hmong toward shingle roofing, especially in Laos. Shingles, depending upon the availability of material, can be made by either splitting logs into shingles, or by lapping pieces of bark.

Laotian Hmong houses also tend to be more substantial than those in Thailand, and at cooler elevations, are built directly on the ground. Many of them are built from thick, hand sawed wooden planks. The vertical posts that support the roof have ritual importance. According to researchers Susanne Bessac and Jo Rainbolt, before a house was built, "grains of rice were placed in small holes where the corners of the house would be, and an egg was placed at the site of the future hearth". If the rice grains remained undisturbed overnight, it was assumed that there were no spiritual objections to the intended construction. Bessac and Rainbolt also report that there was a ritual significance in locating the main door of a Laotian Hmong house. The door was supposed to face "the saddle between two mountain peaks so that good fortune could flow freely to the family".

Nearly all Hmong houses had dirt floors. Salt was periodically sprinkled over the dirt in order to both harden the dirt and reduce the dust. Floors were usually swept at least twice a day. Most houses also contained a vertical post reserved for the house "spirit". Sometimes it was a special center post, and sometimes it was one of the posts otherwise supporting the roof. This post was acknowledged at special ceremonial times of the year, and particularly during naming cermonies.

Very few American Hmong can remember electricity in Laotian homes. Electricity was usually reserved for those Hmong living in close proximity to military installations, where electricity was sporadic at best, and usually supplied by generators. The most common lighting device, for those who could afford it, was an ordinary pressure-pump lantern. Telephones in the home were unheard of.

Interior furnishings were almost always handmade from local, natural materials. Beds tended to be frames constructed from intertwined lengths of split bamboo which were covered with blankets for padding. Woven baskets were an essential part of every household. Some were used for storage containers, while others were used as carrying containers. A special basket was often reserved for the "paj ntaub" family textiles. If the house contained stools, these were often made by tightly coiling mats of sewn rice straw into solid-core bundles. The bundles were secured with bands of hemp or vine. If a house included a loft, the floor of the loft was usually covered with a woven mat. Another interesting characteristic of many Hmong homes in Thailand was the presence of melon and squash vines growing over thatched roofs - a practical way of discouraging livestock from spoiling a harvest.

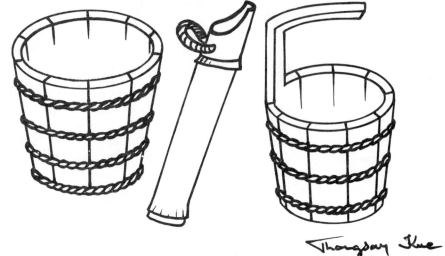

3 types of water containers. Center container is hollow length of bamboo.

Hmong house near military installation, made from discarded 55 gallon oil drums flattened. Drum covers as fencing. Laos.

Elevated chicken and dove houses typical for most Hmong.

A portable Hmong chicken house in North Carolina. In Laos, this form would be woven from bamboo slats.

Cooking customs vary. Many Hmong remember cooking in detached sheds to reduce odors and heat. Others remember cooking at indoor fireplaces. Very often a house contained two fireplaces - one for the preparation of family meals, and the other used for preparing pig chow such as corn and "Sultana Impatients". Almost all Hmong homes, even in the United States, contain a sacred section of wall akin to an altar. This is identified by squares of foil and colored paper that are often bordered along the bottom edge with rooster neck feathers, and drops of dried rooster blood. This altar serves as a protection for crops, livestock, family members, journeys, and overall economic well being.

Another, very unusual house, which is remembered by many American Hmong is the house that was made out of recycled 55 gallon oil drums. These houses tended to cluster around military installations where the drums were either discarded or donated. To recycle the drums, they were split open down the side seam and across the top and bottom seams. The sides were pounded flat into rectangular sheets and recycled as an exterior wall covering. The round drum ends were often used as a decorative fencing to delineate property lines. These were placed with about one-third of the disc buried below ground, and two-thirds left exposed above ground as a fence.

Outbuildings   Outbuildings tended to be either field shelters, animal shelters, or separate cooking sheds. Field shelters (usually a post and thatch construction), were used as a shaded rest area to escape the midday sun, or as a protected area in the event of rain.

Farm animals were usually tethered, rather than allowed to roam free. Tethering was done either by attaching a rope to one of the animal's feet, or by attaching a rope to a ring through the nose, as was the custom with larger animals like water buffalo. Sometimes, in cases of elevated houses, animals were tethered beneath the structure.

In Laos, nearly all Hmong tried to raise their own poultry and doves. In order to discourage predators, and to assist in cleaning, many poultry and dove shelters were elevated off the ground on posts. Sometimes, for scratching and pecking about, the birds were confined in loosely woven domes resembling upside-down baskets. In America, these domes tend to be made from wire instead of the traditional bamboo. Poultry domes are easily portable, can be moved about a farmyard, and can be used as confinement shelters when selling poultry at outdoor markets.

Herbal Folk Remedies

The Hmong have retained an extraordinary hands-on knowledge of how to use both Laotian herbs and other non-domestic plants in the prevention and cure of illness. Less than a decade ago, most American Hmong were still living in Laos, and still directly connected to an agrarian lifestyle. In Laos, herbal remedies were as common to the daily household routine as Mercurochrome and bandages are common to Americans.

Nearly all Hmong family gardens, and particularly the garden of the shaman, contained both medicinal and culinary herbs. Probably, because of the

Split cord carrying technique, north Laos.

shaman's involvement in the prevention and cure of illness, medicinal herbs and other plants have also taken on ritual and spiritual significance. Certain herbs require special procedures for harvest, preparation, and application.

Many of the Hmong herbs now found in the United States were transported from Laos, and are now successfully cultivated in American Hmong family gardens. Propagation depends a lot on climatic conditions being similar to Laos. North Carolina Hmong are fortunate enough to enjoy growing conditions comparable with Laos. Hmong herb gardens in North Carolina vary from tiny outdoor plots of only a few plants, to wide varieties of plants carefully tended in greenhouse conditions.

Many crossovers exist between Laotian and North American herbs, but there are also many differences. A lot of the herbs imported from Laos are not easily recognizeable, and to be fair to the botanist, reliability often requires observing plants in their several stages of growth - including greening, flowering, and seed stages. Thus far, we are only aware of very limited botanical observation. Identification is further complicated by language - the Hmong know their own herbs, but they can seldom translate this identification into either English or Latin.

In preparing this text, I've visited a number of Hmong herb gardens...taking cuttings for identification, as well as bringing knowledgeable botanists into these gardens. We've thus far managed to responsibly identify about 65% of what we've found. Our identification represents only the most common plants and is offered only as a record of information. We cannot risk an endorsement of effectiveness. For those readers wishing to know more, we recommend direct contact with knowledgeable Hmong families.

Day Lily: Many Hmong believe the Day Lily is one of the most potent plants in nature. It is used in tea form as a remedy for infertility. Our shaman source says to gather the leaves in full sun, around noon, when the leaves contain the most medicine. In demonstrating the process, our shaman source took great care with how he picked the leaves - each leaf being picked to a different length. The leaves are placed in lukewarm water (not boiling water), and steeped for tea.

Mint: This plant is used to relieve nose bleeds and to assist with blood coagulation. Many people also remember using it to relieve stomach gas.

Smartweed (Polygonum):   As well as using it as a flavoring for beef, many people use it as a poultice to prevent infection on skin sores.

Comfrey: Comfrey is used in healing bone fractures. It is wrapped in leaf form over the fracture, against the skin, and under the splint.

74   **Dock**:   Dock is used in poultice form as a remedy for rash and skin cancers.

Sedum: Sedum is used as a remedy for spells of dizziness. The Hmong often chop it, beat it, and serve it as a garnish on, or with eggs.

Chrysanthemum: This is one of several plants used separately and in combination to build blood. It's a bit of a "tired blood" stimulant and is often mixed into a chicken stuffing before serving.

Mugwort: Mugwort is used in leaf form and is wrapped around ankles and wrists to relieve swelling and fever.

Euphorbia: This plant is used as a relief for heart attack.

Ground Ivy: Clumps of Ground Ivy are wadded together and pressed against the abdomen for relief of problems related to the appendix.

Rue: A small piece of Rue can be placed directly in the ear to relieve earaches. Rue leaves can also be bruised, squeezed to extract the liquid, and then the extract applied directly to the aching area.

Yarrow: Steep Yarrow into a tea in order to relieve problems of bronchitis, choking, and related problems of excessive mucus. Yarrow can also be used to relieve swollen or bleeding gums.

Houttuynia Cordata: When mixed with chrysanthemum, this herb is baked into a chicken stuffing and used to help build the blood.

Balsam: The Balsam seed is steeped in water to make a tea. The tea is ingested to induce or accelerate labor.

Datura: Used as a heart medicine.

Kalanchoe (Airplant):   In poultice form, this herb is used to reduce swelling. In tea form, it is also used as a cure for infertility.

Perilla Frutescens (Tia-to):   When mashed and softened in water, this plant is used as a poultice to reduce swelling. It is also used in meat preparation as both a seasoning and tenderizer.

Japanese Knotweed: By bruising the leaves, steeping them in lukewarm water, and then drinking the tea, this Polygonum is used to relieve constipation.

Ginseng: Many American Hmong families still steep Ginseng root in pure grain alcohol as a type of stimulant, or "tonic", especially to be used by the elderly. It is taken at mealtime as an appetite stimulant, and an overall "lift". In earlier times in Laos, there are stories that a similar stimulant was made with a blend of herbs, alcohol, and bile or spleen (we're not sure which). There are also many reports that Ginseng was used as an aphrodisiac. Recent reports indicate, however, that this practice is being "officially" discouraged.

Opium Poppy: In earlier times, before the Hmong immigrated to America, an extract from the Opium Poppy was sometimes used by the elderly as a pain reliever, especially in geographically isolated environments where no "outside" medical help was immediately available. The Opium Poppy was also used as a means of barter.

Other Stimulants: For the most part, American Hmong live lifestyles unencumbered by chemical dependency. There is little use of alcohol, and only minimal use of tobacco. A woman who smokes would be considered an undesirable life partner.

Fishing and Hunting

The Hmong from north Laos, particularly those who live in mountain regions, do not fish with the typical lowland, Laotian and Thai dip net. On the contrary, because highland waters tend to run faster and are more shallow, northern Hmong either fish by hand grabbing, or they fish in quantity by damming up sections of stream, diverting waters into controlled channels, and then employing the use of elongated, handwoven bamboo fish traps.

The "hneeg", or crossbow is the traditional Hmong weapon for hunting birds and small animals. The stock is hand carved from hardwood. A shallow groove is cut along the length of the stock in which to rest a single arrow. Braided bands of

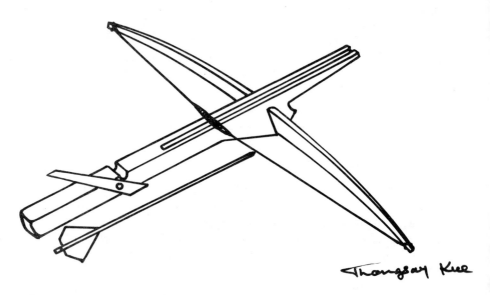

76

"Neev", Hmong crossbow.

rattan or other plant material are used as structural reinforcement where the bow crosses the stock. Before stringing the bow, the string fibers are thoroughly dampened in order to produce the necessary stretch required for stringing. Hmong are incredibly accurate with the crossbow. In northern Thailand, I have personally witnessed this accuracy in target demonstrations where arrows repeatedly strike a bullseye at a distance of about 20 yards. Any time one sees a wad of feathers and dried blood stuck to the stock of a crossbow - this announces the hunter's accuracy.

"Miao" from north Thailand carves crossbow arrow.

Other methods of hunting include game traps, slingshots, and flintlock rifles. According to Dr. Amy Catlin, and author Jean Mottin, the Hmong first came into possession of the flintlock as far back as 1682 when they confiscated one from a traveling General in the Chinese region of Guizhou (Kweichow). Reportedly, one group of Hmong later became renowned for making similar versions of the captured flintlock.

Hmong Natural Association Director Kue Chaw can remember flintlocks being used to hunt tigers in his childhood village. The hunting technique was to locate the tiger's path, load the flintlock, prop it up aimed along the path, and tie a trigger trip string from the trigger to the center of the path in front of the barrel. As the tiger walked along its path in the direction of the flintlock, it tripped the trigger string and shot itself. Kue Chaw can remember that hunters were very careful to post warning signs along the path to warn villagers about the flintlock trap. North Carolina shaman Chu Doua Kue can clearly remember digging in Laotian caves for the natural black powder that was refined into gunpowder.

The Hmong Diet

The pizza, hamburger, French-fry, soft drink, and other fast foods are not included in the traditional Hmong diet, even though many younger American Hmong have quickly adopted these foods. If one word can summarize the Laotian-Hmong diet, that word is "fresh"...and this doesn't mean "fresh-from-the store", or "fresh frozen". It means fresh from the garden or freshly killed.

78   Meat smokehouse stove made from top section of 55 gallon drum.

Hmong are prolific vegetable and herb gardeners, and as often as possible, they raise their own chickens, pigs, doves, and beef (if they can afford beef). They eat fresh fish and enjoy fishing.

The Hmong daily menu is quite different from the menu of an American. Only a minority of Hmong, for example, can ever remember eating a meal comparable to an American "breakfast". Most families were simply too poor to provide a morning meal, and even if one was available, it was nearly identical to the other meals of the day...rice, greens, vegetables, and hopefully a bit of chicken, pork, or fish. "Desserts" were either very rare, or totally unknown. If a "treat" were in the offing for children, it was likely to consist of a small chunk of sugar cane to suck on, or perhaps a finger dipped in honey, or a leaf of mint to chew on to help minimize indigestion.

For the Hmong, the idea of freshness was not only related to food nutrients and taste, but was also a major consideration when the preservation of food, for the most part, was limited to drying, smoking, and salting. Most Hmong households therefore included a meat smokehouse.

One form of smoking stove, familiar to those who lived in proximity to military installations, was made from one-half of a recycled 55 gallon oil drum placed with its open end toward the ground, a smoke hole cut in the top, and a loading door for wood cut into one side. A rack, made with openly spaced warp and weft staves, was suspended above the stove to hold the meat.

Meat for smoke-drying was first cut into thin strips, rubbed with salt, and then draped over the staves of the smoking rack. Smoking usually took at least 24 hours. The dry-smoked meat was then stored on bamboo racks hung from the ceiling. At this point, the meat resembled "jerky". Before it was eaten, it was first boiled, then taken out and pounded, and finally cooked in fresh water with fresh herbs, or the addition of fresh vegetables. Many Hmong can also remember a form of charcoal being used to preserve meat - where meat was placed directly on charcoal, covered, and then allowed to stand. Before it was eventually eaten, the charcoal-cured meat had to be well pounded in order to remove the charcoal taste.

Husking Rice (The "Cu Zev")

One of the commonly embroidered scenes on the contemporary Hmong "paj ntaub" is the husking of rice with a fulcrum device called a "cu zev". The "cu zev" has several parts...a mortar, a mortar cover, a pestle, a pestle shaft and treadle, and the individual pieces that make up the fulcrum. All the pieces are made from hardwood, preferably something like Oak. The mortar and mortar cover are made from a broad, butt log. The cover is made from a lengthwise slice of the mortar log, and the mortar itself is carved into the remainder of the log to a depth of 12-14 inches, and a depression diameter of 10-12 inches. The com-

79

Mao Moua and her sons and daughters prepare to plant rice.

Planting the rice.

Mao Moua and her children use the homemade "cu zev" to begin the process of husking rice.

The mortar, mortar cover, and pestle of the "cu zev".

81

Detail, inside the mortar of the "cu zev".

Mao Moua removes the rice chaff in her "vaab".

pleted mortar is buried in the ground with only about its top 2 inches exposed. The fulcrum for the device consists of vertical posts and a cross member on which the 6-8 foot pestle shaft rests. Another hole is dug in the ground under the treadle end of the pestle shaft in order to allow clearance when the treadle is depressed.

The "cu zev" is most efficiently operated with at least two people...one working the treadle, and the other attending the rice, stirring it, and securing that the pestle manages to husk all the rice kernels. If only one person operates the device, the operator usually ties a rope to the pestle end of the shaft and stretches the rope to where he or she stands on the treadle so that when pressure is applied downward on the treadle, the rope can be pulled to help lift the pestle. The construction of the "cu zev" fulcrum is off center, with most of the weight consequently on the pestle end of the shaft. Adding the rope assists one person in lifting that extra weight.

After the rice has been fully husked, the chaff is then threshed free of the kernel by placing the rice in a flat "vaab", a threshing basket, and tossing the rice in the air, allowing the wind to separate the chaff from the kernel. The Hmong are careful to save the chaff. Many families use chaff as an ingredient with pickled fish in order to accent a salt taste.

Rice husking in Laos is a time of family joy, and is often accompanied by singing and whistling. Children are included in the process and are allowed to sometimes help stand on the treadle or given other responsibilities like discouraging the presence of rice-thieving chickens or small birds during the husking.

"Dlaab tuav ncuav", wooden trough for pounding sticky rice.

Sticky Rice (Ncuav)
by Maytong Kue

Sticky rice is made from a sweet white rice which can be purchased, in this country, from an oriental grocery. It is not the same as a standard white rice. In Laos, the Hmong make sticky rice by crushing it in a hardwood trough, a "dlaab tuav ncuav", which is carved from a log measuring about 30 inches long, by about 14 inches in diameter. The log is cut flat on one side, along its length, so that it can securely rest on the ground during the crushing process. The rice is crushed by two people, each using a long handled, handmade, hardwood mallet called a "dloj tuav ncuav", and using alternate strokes, one mallet up, while the other is down. There is a genuine sense of pride if the mallets are made of one piece construction, and made from wood that has grown naturally bent into mallet shapes (much the same kind of pride a westerner might take upon discovering a naturally bent walking stick).

The rice is pounded in dry form until all lumps disappear, and until the consistency of the pulp is smooth. In this soft form, the pulp can easily spoil, so it should be promptly put to use. The traditional preparation of sticky rice is to form it into patties, and then either fry the patties into fritters, or lightly bake them in the oven until they form a thin, exterior crust. In Laos, the cakes were then eaten after first dipping them in melted sugar cane. In America, Hmong prefer to dip them in honey.

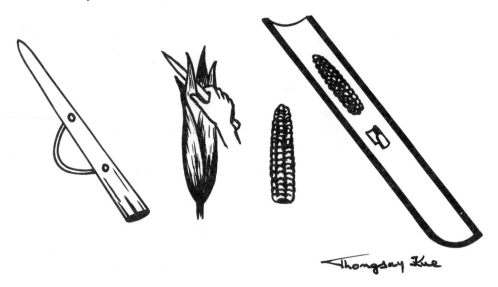

84

Hmong tools for husking corn and removing kernels.

Steamed Fish
by Maytong Kue

With the head and tail intact, and using about 1 tablespoon of cooking oil in a skillet, the fish is first seared on both sides until slightly crisp. Searing helps hold the form of the fish during steaming. The seared fish is then removed from the skillet and basted with either soy sauce or oyster sauce, or a combination of both.

In Laos, the Hmong use sectional bamboo steamers. In America, a light weight metal steamer is more common. The lower section of the steamer is filled, about half full, with water. The fish is placed on a platter or in a shallow bowl, and then placed in the perforated section of the steamer. A garnish of thinly sliced red pepper, onion, and fresh ginger is added before steaming. A sprig of fresh coriander or lemon balm may also be added. The cover is placed securely on the steamer and the fish is steamed from 30-45 minutes, depending upon the size of the fish. The fish is then served from the same platter or bowl used during steaming.

Boiled Chicken

The Hmong prefer fresh chicken, and whenever possible, they will raise and butcher their own. For a boiled chicken dinner, the chicken is boiled for 30-50 minutes, depending upon the size of the bird. It is then removed from the pot, placed on a cutting surface, and chopped right through the bones into pieces measuring about 3 finger widths. These pieces are then placed in a large bowl and garnished with salt, Accent, black pepper, and herbs. The pieces are tossed in the bowl like salad in order to absorb the seasoning. The chicken is served, bones intact, and the individual pieces are often first dipped in hot pepper before eating.

Chicken/Broccoli Stir-fry

To stir-fry, the skin is first removed from the chicken, the meat is cut into long, thin pieces, and then fried, stirring in salt, a bit of cornstarch, Accent, and steak sauce. The sauce is cooked until it begins to thicken, and then pieces of broccoli are added, lightly cooked, and served with the chicken.

Tofu (Without Culture)
by Maytong Kue

Soak about 10 cups of dry soy beans for a long overnight (about 12 hours). In Laos, the beans were then crushed in a "zeb" corn grinder. In America, the beans are placed in a blender until smooth, or about the consistency of whipped cream. This blending is then poured into a cloth bag measuring about 8 inches wide by 12 inches deep. The bag is held directly over a bowl and squeezed, until all the liquid separates from the bean pulp.

85

The pulp is discarded, but the liquid from the bag is saved and boiled about one-half hour, with consistent stirring to avoid scorching. The bag is cleaned. Next, the juice and pulp from about 10 lemons is mixed with 2 cups of water and added to the liquid while hot. This addition is stirred, but not cooked.

The mixture is then placed back in the bag and once again squeezed. What remains in the bag is then placed in a bowl, covered with water to the top of the mixture, covered with plastic wrap, refrigerated, and allowed to stand until it jells into tofu. Some of the water drained from the bag (with the lemon already in it) is saved as a culture for the next recipe of tofu. This eliminates the use of lemons in the next mixture.

Traditional Hmong corn grinder, "zeb".

Greens

Fresh greens, either eaten raw, steamed, or marinated are a staple of the Hmong diet. Greens are usually served in combination with either rice or noodles. Edible greens in the Hmong menu include chard, mustard, spinach, collard, the tender green tops of both pod and snow peas (including the flowers), the unfolding new leaves of pumpkin and squash plants, and the first emerging leaves of the poppy. When greens are steamed, the Hmong often garnish them with fresh coriander.

Marinated Greens

Marinating vinegar is prepared from dry soy beans. The beans are soaked for a long overnight (10-12 hours), and then the soaking liquid and the beans are placed in a blender and blended until smooth. This mixture is then poured into a shallow pan and cooked together with the juice of fresh lemons to taste (increasing the amount of lemon increases the sourness of the marinate). As the mixture boils, it will scum. This scum is skimmed off and saved as an additive to other dishes.

Lightly cooked greens are then placed in a bowl. The marinate, including the bean particles, is next poured over the greens. The bowl is covered, and the greens are allowed to stand in the marinate from 2 to 3 days. When marinated greens are served with rice they are often eaten in combination with hot pepper.

Hmong Fried Rice
(A Festival Dish)

8-10 Servings

Ingredients
1 pound chicken gizzards
1 whole chicken breast, boned and skinned
1 pound medium shrimp, shelled
$\frac{1}{2}$ cup lard or oil
5 large cloves of garlic, minced
6 tablespoons fish sauce (available from oriental grocery)
$\frac{1}{2}$ cup thick soy sauce
$\frac{1}{4}$ cup water
16 cups steamed, cooked rice
1 can (16 ounces) straw mushrooms, drained (or similar quantity of fresh mushrooms)
Tomatoes, cucumbers and scallions, for garnish
1 lime, quartered and sliced

Preparation Trim tough sinews from gizzards with a sharp knife, or if used whole and untrimmed, then boil gizzards about 3 hours. Wash gizzards, chicken and shrimp thoroughly. Slice each meaty portion of gizzard without cutting all the way through in order to create a fan-like effect - then cut crosswise thin slices about half way through - everything held together from one uncut base. Next, cut chicken breast into strips and slit back of shrimp along center and spread open into butterfly. De-vein shrimp.

Using a large (oversized) skillet or wok, first melt the lard or oil and saute garlic with the gizzards over a medium heat until garlic is golden brown. Add

87

chicken, then shrimp. Add fish sauce, the thick soy sauce and the water. Stir fry for 5-7 minutes. Add the rice and mushrooms. If fresh mushrooms are used, these should be added last in order not to overcook. Stir and blend ingredients to distribute sauces thoroughly.

Halve and slice two or more tomatoes and cut two or more peeled and seeded cucumbers into thick, diagonal strips. Use with lime as garnish around fried rice or arrange on a serving plate, along with curled scallion stalks. Scallion stalks are curled by shredding them with a needle into a fringe and then soaking them in cold water until they "fan" out.

Hot Sauce Garnish   For those who wish an extra hot sauce, mash or grind one hot pepper per serving and blend with 5 cloves of minced garlic. Add one teaspoon sugar, three tablespoons of thin fish sauce, one tablespoon soy sauce, and the juice from one lime. After blending ingredients, add one tablespoon minced, fresh coriander.

88   Hmong planting stick for planting seed.

Khaub Poob (Hot Noodles)
by Mai Kue

8 Servings

Ingredients
2 packages, oriental style, thin wheat flour noodles
12 cups water
one-half cup fresh peppermint leaves
one-half medium size cabbage (chopped)
2 tablespoons chili paste with garlic (available from oriental grocery)
one-half chicken
1 can bamboo shoots
one-half cup coconut milk (either fresh or canned)

Preparing Noodles Boil water in a 4 quart saucepan, then add one package of noodles, and cook for 7-8 minutes. Do not pour noodles out of saucepan. Noodles should be cooled by adding cold water and then draining off only the water. Remove noodles with thumb and forefinger and place them on a strainer or rack to dry. Repeat procedure for second package.

Preparing Chicken Stew the chicken about 30 minutes in a medium size stewing pan (save the broth). Remove the chicken from the broth and remove all meat from

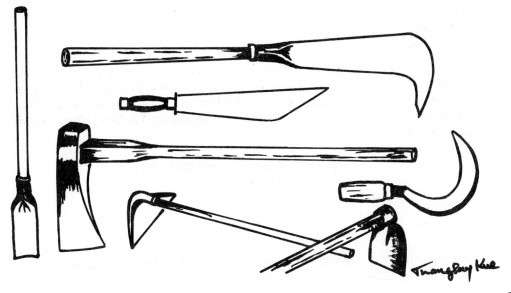

Typical Hmong hand tools used with agriculture and other chores.

89

bones. Remove any scum from broth. Replace the meat back into the broth and add the 2 tablespoons of chili paste with garlic, the coconut milk, and the can of bamboo shoots after first slicing the bamboo shoots into thin strips. Cook the ingredients together over medium to low heat for 10-12 minutes.

Serving Chicken sauce is served hot over noodles. Chopped cabbage and peppermint leaves can either be individually served on each plate, or placed in a serving bowl so that each person can serve themselves. Some people prefer to sprinkle the cabbage and peppermint on top of the chicken - others prefer to place it at the side.

Mov Kua Dlis Gaab Ntsev (Chicken Rice Soup)
by Mai Kue

5-8 Servings

Ingredients
one-half chicken
one and one-half cups long grain rice
one medium size green onion or scallion
1 teaspoon ground black pepper
1 tablespoon salt
1 tablespoon Accent or MSG
1 tablespoon soy sauce
15 cups water

Preparation Boil chicken in medium size saucepan about 30 minutes. Remove the chicken from the broth and remove meat from bones. Remove all scum from broth. Place the chicken meat back in the broth, chop up the onion, add the remaining ingredients, and cook one hour over medium to low heat. Garnish with lemon grass.

Mov Kua Dlis Tsuag (No Salt Soup)
by Mai Kue

4-6 Servings

Ingredients
6 cups water
2 bunches (handfuls) of snowpeas (including leaves and vines), or substitute
    with 2 handfuls chopped cabbage

90   *Preparation* Cook ingredients about 20 minutes and serve.

Tuav Qaub (Lettuce Or Salad Dip)
by Mai Kue

7-9 Servings

Ingredients
15 fresh, grated carrots
4 fresh tomatoes (cut into pieces)
1 head of lettuce or bunch of leaf lettuce
1 teaspoon shrimp paste (available from oriental grocery)
1 teaspoon salt
1 teaspoon Accent or MSG
1 tablespoon fish sauce (available from oriental grocery)
1 teaspoon ground hot pepper or 5 fresh hot peppers
5 cloves garlic
ceramic or stone mortar and pestle, or something similar

Preparation and serving   Ingredients are crushed and blended into a dip by using the mortar and pestle, beginning first with garlic cloves, then adding the carrots, tomatoes and other ingredients. Do not add the lettuce. The lettuce is used like a chip, in the fingers, to scoop up the dip after all ingredients have been smoothly blended.

Pig intestines (left) dried and ready to stuff. The coil on the right side is already stuffed.

Nyuv Ntxwm (Rice Sausage Stuffing)
by Mai Kue

5-8 Servings

Ingredients
2 cups regular or sticky rice
one-half chicken
1 tablespoon salt
one and one-half teaspoons Accent or MSG
10 cups water
2 inches fresh ginger root
5 lengths pork intestine, 18 inches long (can be substituted by using banana
    leaves)

Preparation   Soak rice overnight. Stew chicken in 10 cups water adding seasoning while it cooks. After chicken is done, cool it for ten minutes and remove all
meat from bones. Chop meat into small pieces and add it to the rice. Tie off one
end of sausage liner. Using a funnel, pour chicken broth into liner, and then add
the mixture of rice and meat. Do not try to stuff the rice and meat first. Pouring in
the broth first makes it much easier to add the rice and meat mixture. After the
liner is full, tie off the open end. Using a double boiler, steam the stuffed sausage
for about 30 minutes, or until done. Do not place the sausage in the water. In
Laos, when intestine liner was not available, banana leaves were often substituted. An intestine for stuffing is simply washed, then sun dried.

Fawm Kauv (Rice Wrapper)
by Mai Kue

10-12   Servings

Note: This recipe consists of 3 parts: wrapper, stuffing, and dip.

Wrapper   In a medium size bowl, blend 3 cups flour, 1 cup corn starch, 1
tablespoon vegetable oil and 5 cups water. Next, add ingredients to an electric
blender and blend until smooth. The wrapper batter is cooked similarly to a
crepe, and is round, about 7-8 inches in diameter, and very thin. Cook the
wrapper batter on a non-stick fry pan. Heat the pan and ladle in about one
serving spoonful of batter. Swirl the batter around so that it covers the bottom of
the pan. Pour off any excess batter. If the batter is thin enough, the wrapper
should cook through without flipping.

92

Stuffing   2 pounds finely chopped and cooked chicken or pork. 2 medium size green onions, finely chopped. Add 1 tablespoon vegetable oil to a medium size pan, place over moderate heat, and add the meat, the onions, and 1 teaspoon of both salt and Accent or MSG. Simmer and blend ingredients. After cooked, spoon about one heaping tablespoon of stuffing onto wrapper, spread, and roll up wrapper from one end to the other.

Dip   Blend 1 teaspoon Accent or MSG with 3 tablespoons of oriental fish sauce or soy sauce, one-half teaspoon sugar, 1 teaspoon ground hot pepper (optional), and 2 tablespoons of chopped peanuts (also optional). Squeeze the juice from two slices of fresh lemon and blend into the dip.

Serving   The stuffed wrapper is eaten with fingers, adding just a tad of dip to taste.

Grubs, Grasshoppers, Cicadas, and Bee Larvae

In Laos, the Hmong regularly include grubs, grasshoppers, cicadas, and bee larvae as a part of their diet. Two types of grubs, for example, live in the bamboo plant - one in the stalk and leaves of the plant, and the other which clusters at the base. The grubs are gathered when they are plump. Like grasshoppers and cicadas, the grubs are roasted, and have a nut-like taste and consistency.

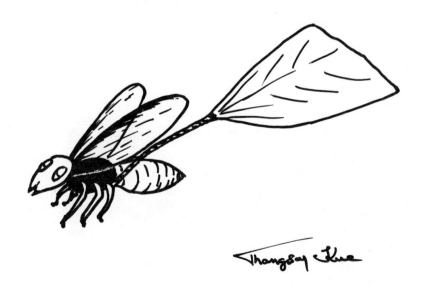

Chicken feather looped around bee in order to locate honey.

93

Bee larvae are steamed, rather than roasted. These too, have a nut-like taste. Many of the Laotian Hmong in America can remember being involved in the excitement of bee hunts. One of the most interesting recollections involves attracting a bee to a piece of deliberately placed meat, lassoing the bee with a loop of yarn or hair that has been tied to a white, chicken breast feather, and then tracing the bee's return flight to its hive by posting family members at surrounding critical locations in the forest. What happens is that the bee becomes preoccupied with eating the meat bait, and before it realizes what has happened, the hunter has looped the bee with a feather lasso. Care has to be taken to make certain that the weight of the feather does not prevent the bee from becoming airborne.

Once the bee hive is located, the hunters return, usually at night, employ smoke to stun the bees, open the hive, and then remove the larvae. If the hive is underground, the hunter blows smoke from a torch into the hive opening. Larvae hunting is usually done in September when the larvae are plump. Once a hive has been located, the hunter sets up rice straw bundles around the hive. These bundles notify others in the area that the encircled hive has been claimed.

Bees in Laos reportedly produce larger larvae than those in the United States. Many American Hmong have sampled bee larvae in this country, but claim that these larvae are too small to eat.

Testing Wild Mushrooms

According to tradition, the way to test whether or not wild mushrooms are poisonous, is to cook them with rice. If the rice turns red, the mushrooms are assumed to be poisonous. We cannot, however, guarantee this as a "foolproof" test. There have been reports where Hmong in America have been poisoned by wild mushrooms. We do not know if these folks bothered to test their mushrooms ahead of time.

Fumigating For Mice, Rats, and Snakes

At least once a year, or as often as needed, many Hmong still burn hot peppers under their houses in order to ward off rodents and snakes. This is done by placing a quantity of dried peppers in a metal pan, setting the pan under the house, igniting the peppers, and then closing off the air supply under the house so that the smoke remains trapped for as long as possible.

Children and Their Games

A typical Hmong household is a roof offering protection for people. It's a space bursting with vitality. It's a mini-universe of sound, smell, movement, contact, compromise, and caring. To a westerner, what might otherwise appear to be several families in quantity...is probably nothing more than one extended Hmong family living more or less harmoniously under one roof. This collection of members can include more than one adult female (if the adult male has more than one wife), it can include grandparents (sometimes both paternal and maternal grandparents), and it can include aunts, uncles, and usually lots of children, many of whom may be very close in age.

Each child, within a Hmong household, is therefore a vital, functioning part of a totality. The Hmong do not look upon childhood as some sort of disconnected "nowhere land" where children exist in "limbo" while awaiting adulthood. On the contrary, each child within a family shares a measure of very real responsibility. Children play an important part in the sharing of family workload - and this might be in the form of babysitting a younger family member, preparing food, cooking, gardening, tending animals, or even instructing younger family members with their school lessons, or with learning their family responsibilities.

Intergenerational contact is likely to be an everyday experience in a Hmong household. The typical Hmong family does not pack up their "Little Red Riding Hood" and send her off to visit her grandmother. On the contrary, the child is likely to see her grandmother all the time. Grandmother is an everyday reality who shares, teaches, entertains, disciplines, and hugs. Grandmother and grandfather are greatly respected. They do not outlive their usefulness. Age, and aging are not abstractions for the Hmong child.

In Laos, most Hmong families try to be as self-sufficient as possible. As in all cultures, self-sufficiency is labor intensive. A lot of work goes into living. In the spring of 1986, I participated with an American Hmong family of 10 members in planting a 5 acre field of rice (previously plowed) in less than 3 hours time. With busy hoes and rakes, we were a substantial labor force of children, parents, and grandparents working together on a family project with a practical, non-abstract purpose...namely, real rice for real people. That same field might have taken as long as 2 or 3 days to plant if the planting had been the sole responsibility of only the parents.

In visiting dozens of Hmong households during the research for this book, I have many times been present when exhausted parents returned home from boring-to-mediocre factory jobs in America to find dinner already cooked, the table set, chores attended to, and a sizeable share of the logistics for family life

95

Hmong children of the Morganton housing project.

Hmong rubber band jumprope.

already cared for by children of all ages…without complaint, and as a normal, non-spectacular contribution to a family.

Childhood, however, is not all work. It's also a supportive, joyful time of play and normal make-believe. It's a time for games, riddles, contests, and toys. In Laos, however, children seldom have contact with the world of manufactured games and toys. Laotian Hmong have inherited a tradition of improvising by hand in order to make whatever props or equipment become necessary in play. In Laos, the imagination of the child has not yet been rendered extinct by commerce.

Rubberband Jumprope By doubling and looping rubber bands together, Hmong children chain an elastic cord, which can measure up to 10 feet in length, depending upon how many bands are chained. Two children hold the out-stretched band, one on either end, while a third child either jumps or cartwheels over the band. Each time a jump is successful, the band is lifted higher and higher in a horizontal plane, until the jumper's feet finally touch the band. Touching the band ends the turn and makes room for another jumper.

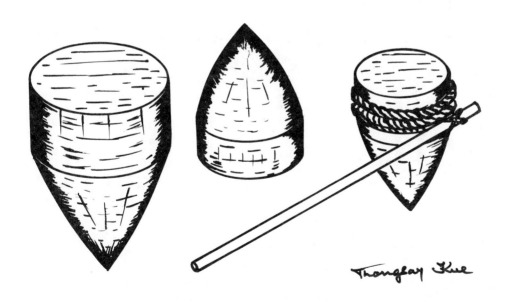

Handmade "tuaj lub", string and top.

"Tuaj Lub" or Top Spinning   "Tuaj Lub" consists of a wooden top, a thin, flat stick about one yard in length, and a length of ordinary string. The game is played all year, but has special interest during the New Year celebration. String is wrapped around the top and the top is spun off the stick. Many players participate at one time. Seeming a bit like "carom", each player is encouraged to hit another player's top with one's own. The player whose top remains spinning the longest wins the game.

"Ntaus Ntiv" or Paddle Game   A "bird" or "Tis Qab" is made from either a dry, shucked corncob, or a short piece of bamboo. 3 or 4 fairly large chicken feathers protrude out from the "Tis Qab". These feathers cause the "Tis Qab" to wobble and spin when hit. The point of the game is to hit the "Tis Qab" with a wooden paddle called a "Dluav", and to see how long the "Tis Qab" can remain airborne. The player who allows it to hit the ground loses the game.

"Ntaus ntiv", paddle game with "tis qab" bird.

"Ua Txwv" or Pebble Jacks   This game is similar to American "Jacks" except that it is played with small pebbles, and without a ball. The players begin with up to 10 pairs, or a total of 20 small pebbles. The point of the game is to use one hand, toss the pebbles carefully in the air in increasing numbers, and catch as many as possible, using the same hand. The player who catches the most pebbles wins the game.

Guessing Games   Hmong children play a version of guessing game similar to "Guess Which Hand"...a game which uses kernels of corn transferred from one hand to the other with both hands hidden behind the back. The player who guesses must guess which hand holds the kernels. A second version of the same guessing game is to guess the exact number of corn kernels held in the hand.

Children also play guessing games as riddles, where one child gives verbal clues to a riddle, and the other children try to guess the answer. The player who guesses the correct answer wins a turn at making up the next riddle.

The telling of wizard stories is yet another favorite form of children's entertainment. Sometimes these stories are joined by adults and can last up to an hour or more, with an audience encouraging the storyteller to complicate and embroider the plot.

Of Interest To Boys   Hmong boys play a game called "Ntiv Txiaj", which is a mix between "hackysack" and soccer. Shin guards are made by wrapping animal skins around the legs, below the knees, and padding the shins with corncob husks. From between 5 to 10 doughnut-like Laotian pennies are tied together with string and chicken feathers. The result of all this is an object resembling a "feathered hackysack" which is then kicked.

Another traditional favorite of boys is to organize beetle fights with either cow-dung or bamboo beetles. The boys scoop out a narrow trench in the ground, place two beetles in the trench headed toward each other, and hope for a fight. Another version of the same contest is make a leash for the beetles by threading a length of long hair through the insect's hide, and then urging the beetle into combat via the leash.

"Nkauj Nyaab" or Corncob Doll   "Nkauj Nyaab" is a corncob doll made for girls. Usually the doll has both a mouth and eyes poked into the cob with the tip of a knife. Corn silk is sewn onto the cob to resemble hair. The doll does not have to have arms or legs.

Other Forms   Like children the world over, the Hmong remember making wet clay, or "mudpie" figures. The most common forms were goats, cows, chicken, and horses. Animal toys were also made by piecing together lengths of bamboo.

Hmong/Laotian Expressions And Proverbs

Don't grow rice on our backs! Refers to those who would exploit, expecially those who would exploit the Hmong.

Be careful eating chicken leg! A caution, usually reserved for young men, suggesting that a young man may be unable to catch the girl he wants if he loses his claws.

Hmong time. A joke, usually expressed to Americans, to let them know that Hmong are very often late, especially for meetings.

Don't look me higher than your ankle! Often said if someone makes you unhappy or angry.

Be careful not to hit your head on a dead tree branch, or poke your eye with a dead branch! Take care when complaining about others for fear of making your own mistakes.

An elephant's foot can strike a small bird. A warning of self caution when exercising power over others.

One stick cannot build a house.

A tiger may have spots outside, but man has them inside!

A table may have feet, but it cannot walk!

Just because a chicken dies outside the house is no reason for everyone to pray!

When a man sharpens his knife, everyone thinks it's time to eat!

What you put in your mouth returns on your stomach!

The chicken is stuck in a hole. Refers to a woman who has snagged an earring.

Hit the dog's tail and the dog cries. Refers to the foot pedal on the traditional Hmong device for winnowing rice.

It's time to shoot the arrow! An expression a father tells his son when it is time for the son to leave the home.

One stick cannot cook a meal, or build a fence.

One man cannot build a country!

Those who do not unite do not survive!

Thirteen rules in the kitchen, fourteen rules in the house. Refers to the male Hmong responsibility for the broader perspective.

A sharp blade with two sides. A person who takes both sides of the same argument.

What stands on both sides of the hill and just fits when you jump? Answer: *Pants!*

What is it that's like a jungle with children on its back? Answer: *Corn!*

Butterfly. This is often a synonym for money - many butterflies in the life referring to good times and sufficient money.

Tiger doesn't eat tiger. A political expression from Laos, meaning that if a Hmong has a problem with a Lao, he shouldn't expect sympathy from another Lao. Similar meaning for Hmong in America except the American is now substituted for the Lao.

Hmong Stories and Songs

Oral tradition, as expressed in both stories and songs, has been one of the means by which the Hmong have preserved their ancient culture. We offer the following in printed form, knowing full well that much has been lost, both in translation, and because live performance is missing. How much better it would be to share these stories and songs by adding the richness of the human voice as well as the animation of the individual performer. Hopefully, the following will add yet another dimension into understanding the subtleties of Hmong folklife.

Origins And Why The First Inhabitants Of Laos Will Never Drown In The Nam Et River

(As told by Mua Cha and thanks to Susanne Bessac and Jo Rainbolt)

There were 3 brothers living in a small settlement of only 3 houses. One night, one of the brothers had a very vivid dream. A young man came to him in his sleep and said: "I need help from you. Please come tomorrow morning with your arrows. Come to the big rock by the side of the river and wait for me. I am going to marry the River King's youngest daughter, but she has another suitor and he will fight for her hand with me. I am not sure I can win, so I need help from you. You will see 2 dragons. The green-headed dragon is me. Do not shoot it. If the red-headed dragon is on top, shoot it."

All night the brother lay awake wondering why he had experienced such a dream. He asked his wife: "Should I go to the rock, or not?" Finally, just before dawn, when it was still quite dark, he got up, took his crossbow and arrows, walked to the big rock and waited. At first light, when he could still not see very clearly, he heard a noise and saw the waters of the river churn, rise up high, and then ebb away. The water rose again. This time much higher, and then it was that he saw the red-headed dragon, and the red-headed dragon was on top. "My dream told me the truth", he said. So he aimed his arrow carefully, and shot. The red-headed dragon sank from sight.

On the next night, the young man in the previous night's dream appeared again in another dream. He said: "I am so happy you helped me. From now on, you may fish and go anywhere on this river, south to north, and I will help you. Anything you need I will bring you. I will never let your people die in this river. I am now King of this river, all of it, and the fish of this river are for you to catch."

3 days later the brother decided to test the river. He put a 3 day old baby in the river. The baby did not sink. The river water gently supported the baby.

The dragons of the rivers have scales which shimmer blue, red, and purple. When the sunlight reflects off of them, it creates a rainbow. That's why Hmong people say that rainbows are dragon snakes. Dragon snakes are dangerous for Hmong people and that's why the Hmong fear the rainbow.

"Paj Ntaub", Flower Cloth Tiger Story One

Many years ago, a man killed a gibbon, but a tiger was looking and saw the man, so the tiger killed the man and ate him. The tiger took the man's clothes and put them on. He took the man's gun, and then went to the man's house.

The tiger said to the man's wife: "I am your husband". The wife believed him. She didn't know he was a tiger.

But the wife had a younger sister named Yer. Yer knew the tiger was not a man. Yer climbed upstairs in the house and hid. That night, the tiger ate the wife and all the children. "Crunch, Crunch!". Yer remained hidden, but she heard the "crunch, crunch" and was frightened.

The next morning the tiger asked Yer to come down. Yer was afraid, but she didn't come down. She threw hot pepper in the tiger's eyes. The tiger had to go to the river to wash out his eyes.

While he was gone, Yer spoke to a bird and asked the bird to fly to her family and tell them that a tiger had eaten her older sister and all the children. She asked the bird to bring her family right away, so the bird flew away and delivered the message. Yer's family came immediately. They asked Yer where the tiger had gone. "He's down at the river washing pepper out of his eyes", answered Yer. "I'll call him now...TIGER, TIGER", called Yer. "My family is here. They want to talk to you. Come now, and I'll be your wife".

"Good", answered the tiger. So he started back along the path toward the house, but Yer's brothers had dug a deep hole exactly in the middle of the path. They covered the hole with leaves. The two brothers met the tiger as he approached. The three continued walking toward the house, but the brothers made sure the tiger walked right over the leaves and fell in the hole. The brothers killed him.

Variations Of Tiger Story One

Same man goes out to hunt. He spots a gibbon in a tree, shoots it dead, but the gibbon doesn't fall. It gets hung up in the tree. A tiger comes along and tells the man that if he wants to get the gibbon out of the tree, he'd be better off to climb the tree without his clothes on. So the man agrees with the suggestion, takes off his clothes and climbs the tree. While he's up there, the tiger puts on the man's clothes, and takes his gun. The man comes down with the gibbon, and the tiger even steals the gibbon away.

Later, wearing the man's clothes, carrying his gun, and carrying the dead gibbon, the tiger goes to the man's house and poses as the husband. The man has two daughters. When it's time to eat, the tiger cuts the gibbon up into four pieces. The wife cooks three of the pieces, but the tiger prefers to eat his piece raw. Only then does the wife discover that the tiger is not her husband. She knows her husband only eats cooked gibbon.

Still another variation of the same story is about a sick man who says to his wife that if he dies, he wants to be buried under his own house. The man dies. The wife does as she was asked and buries her husband under the house. The wife continues to live in the house, to spin her yarn, and to make "paj ntaub" (flower cloth). Meanwhile, the dead husband turns into a tiger, comes up out of the ground, chases his wife out of the house, and eats two of his own children. The wife runs to her parents, she tells them about the tiger, and the father shoots the tiger.

Tiger Story Two

(Recorded by David C. Graham in "Songs and Stories of the Ch'uan Miao", Washington, D.C. Smithsonian Miscellaneous Collection, 1954)

There were three brothers who saw a huge water buffalo feeding on the other side of a river. One of the brothers said to the other two: "If you will put this basket on my head (baskets often seem to have magic qualities; other stories tell of large rice winnowing baskets being used as wings to enable a man to fly), I will cross the river and fetch the water buffalo for you, but you must promise to later take the basket off my head again".

The brothers agreed and gave their promise. They placed the basket on the one brother's head. Promptly, he changed into a mighty tiger, easily swam across the river, grabbed the buffalo, and dragged it back to the two waiting brothers. Try as they may, the two brothers were unable to get the basket off the third brother's head. The third brother remained a tiger.

Later, when one of the brothers (who was not very popular) wanted to become head man of the village, he called out the name of his tiger brother, which the tiger could hear, no matter how far away he might be. Other people however, never dared pronounce the name for fear the tiger brother would appear at once and eat them.

"Brother, help me to become head man of the village", said the unpopular brother to the tiger. So the tiger tyrannized the villagers until they made his brother head man. This tiger would still be terrorizing the countryside had it not been that he forgot himself one day while babysitting his brother's children, and happened to eat one of the children. His other two brothers killed him with a silver bullet.

Other Tiger Story Variations

Several writers believe that at one time during their long history, the Hmong may have had something akin to a "tiger cult". Sometimes there are stories where the tiger becomes the hero, as well as the villain.

One of these variations describes where a tiger goes to visit a sick boy. The tiger offers to take the boy on a tour of the village and the countryside. While they're gone, the tiger asks the boy to play him a song on the "geej" (free reed mouth organ). The boy not only agrees, but decides to teach the tiger how to play. Finally, after wonderful adventures and friendship, the two return home with the boy riding on the back of his friend, the tiger.

Flood Story
(The Origin Of Hmong Names)

Long ago, a lot of water fell from the sky. Water was over the houses, over the trees, and water was everywhere. In the water was a drum. It was wood. It floated in the water. There were two people in the drum - a brother and a sister. No father, no mother, no babies, no chickens, no pigs, no oxen, no buffalo, no horses, no insects, no squirrels, and no birds. Only two people - one brother and one sister.

One day the water decreased. The drum stopped floating. It finally touched the ground, and the boy and girl stepped out of the drum. The girl asked: "Where are all the people?" "Dead", answered the boy. "The animals are also dead". The girl then said: "No people, no animals, only you and only me".

The brother and sister were sad. The boy said: "Marry me, and we can have children. We can make more people". But the sister wouldn't listen. She said: "I cannot marry you. You are my brother". Then the next day, the brother once again asked his sister to marry him, but the sister refused. Every day the brother asked again and again.

So, after many days of asking, the girl said: "Brother, you throw a stone down the mountain, and I'll throw a stone down the mountain. I don't think the stones will come back up the mountain, but if they do, I'll agree to marry you".

So the boy threw his stone and the girl threw her stone. That same night, the boy climbed down the mountain. The night was dark. The boy carried his stone back up the mountain and placed it on the grass. Then he went back down the mountain again and carried his sister's stone back up the mountain and placed it next to his own stone on the grass. The next day he called to his sister: "Come, look, the stones came back up the mountain. Now they are together. Now you can marry me".

So the brother and sister were married. They were husband and wife. After awhile they had a baby. The baby was round like a stone. It had no arms and no legs, so they cut the baby into many pieces and threw the pieces away. Each of the pieces made new people. Some of the pieces landed in the garden, so those new people were named "Vang", because "Vang" sounded very much like "garden" in Hmong.

104

Other pieces fell in the weeds and grass, so those new people were named "Thao", because "Thao" sounded very much like "weeds and grass" in Hmong. Still other pieces fell on top of the goat house, so those new people were named "Lee" which sounded like "goat house". Other pieces fell on top of the pig house, so those new people were named "Moua", because "Moua" sounded like "pig house" in Hmong.

By the very next day, every family had a house, chickens, pigs, oxen, buffaloes, and horses. There were insects, squirrels, and birds. The brother and sister looked at each other and said: "Now we are no longer sad. We are not alone anymore".

(Thanks to Barry G. Huffman).

Shee Na And Ngao Njua

Shee Na had a beautiful wife. Her name was Ngao Njua. A very rich man wanted Ngao Njua, so he took her away. The rich man said to her: "You are my 8th wife". This made Ngao Njua very sad, so she cried. Shee Na also cried.

All this crying made the sky cloudy and rainy. The rich man said: "Ngao Njua will not smile". Then Shee Na said: "I'm going to go and find Ngao Njua. I'm going to bring her home". So he took his good clothes off and put on animal skins. He took along his "geej". He walked a very long way in search of the rich man's house, but finally he found it.

Shee Na looked up at the window where Ngao Njua lived and then he played upon his "geej". Ngao Njua heard the sounds and understood their meaning. She looked out her window and smiled.

The rich man saw her smile. He said: "Ngao Njua smiled. I didn't make her smile. Who made her smile?" So he looked out his window and saw a man wearing animal skins. The rich man went outside and said to Shee Na: "I would like to buy your clothes. I want to make my wife smile". So he bought the animal skins and put them on. In the meanwhile, Shee Na put on the rich man's clothes.

But the dogs smelled the animal skins. They jumped on the rich man and killed him. The rich man had two sons. The sons came home. Shee Na said to Ngao Njua: "I am afraid the rich man's sons will kill us". So Shee Na and Ngao Njua ran away. They ran and ran. The rich man's sons ran after them. The sons came to a village. They asked: "Did you see a man and a woman?" The villagers replied: "Yes, very early this morning, at the rooster's first crow, they went that way". So the sons went in the same direction.

They chased Shee Na and Ngao Njua. They came to a second village and asked: "Did you see a man and a woman?". The people answered: "Yes, very early this morning, at the rooster's first crow, and they went that way". So the sons went in the same direction. They came to a third village and asked the same question: "Did you see a man and a woman?". And once again, they received the same answer: "Yes, very early this morning, at the rooster's first crow, they went that way".

But by now the sons were very tired. They said: "We can't seem to catch them. We don't know where they are. Let's go home!" So the sons went home.

Shee Na and Ngao Njua ran for many days. Every night they stopped. They ate and slept. They made pots for cooking, but they could not carry the pots. They always left the pots behind. And every night they made more pots.

Our grandparents say: "Go to the plain of jars in Laos. You will see some big jars. These jars are the pots of Shee Na and Ngao Njua. Shee Na and Ngao Njua made them a long time ago".

(Thanks to Barry G. Huffman).

The Monkeys at Grasshopper Hill

The monkeys went to grasshopper hill. They said: "You grasshoppers! You killed our cousin!"

"We did not", the grasshoppers said.

"Yes you did", replied the monkeys, "and we're going to fight you!"

So the grasshoppers said: "My goodness, it's too early in the morning. Why don't you wait a little while. Wait until the sun comes up and warms us".

So the monkeys waited. The sun came up. The grasshoppers got good and warm, so they hopped up on top of the monkeys' heads. This made the monkeys very angry, so they got big sticks. They wanted to kill the grasshoppers, so they hit their own heads hard. Very hard!

But they didn't kill a single grasshopper. The grasshoppers just hopped away.

(Thanks to Barry G. Huffman).

Love song
(Translation by Lao Toua Lo)

Which is the flower that blooms like a spring bride?
It is the peachtree flower.

If I marry you one day,
I'll bring you with me to paradise.
You'll have everything you need.
I'll find you a market, and you can shop until
your heart's content.

Lament
Upon Leaving Our Country

(Song by Doua Her for parents, family, cousins, and friends. This version is not a literal translation. It is an edited English adaptation with the help of Thongsay Kue)

The leader of our people wrote a letter to the opposition.
He told how our country was large.
How there was room enough for everyone.
He asked the opposition to divide and share the land.
He wrote how it takes more than grass and trees to make a country.
How it takes people.
Our country is like a great bridge joining people together.
If the bridge breaks, the country will fall apart.
The leader of the opposition took no interest.
So the leader of our people left the country.
All the people cried.
The opposition took over everything.
Our leader took a boat and left his people.
All the people cried.
Some of the people followed their leader.
It was not easy.
The leader of our people traveled to another place.
Even though the new land was good, our leader could not forget.
He remembered his people.
He remembered leaving them behind.
He remembered them crying like chicks without a mother.
He remembered them like chicks without a nest.

Our country has conflict.
This is why we left.
The way we left was not easy.
We walked a lot.
We walked many nights.
We took boats in the night.
We had so little money.
The boatmen needed a lot of money to save our lives.
Some of us went alone.
We left our parents behind.
We cry alone...remembering our parents...our country.   107

If only we could make magic.
If only we could turn into butterflies.
If only we could fly back to see our loved ones…our country.

Our country has conflict.
This is why we left.
Even though we have a new land and new ways, our hearts fly like the eagle for our families left behind.
The young girl asks the young boy about his family left behind.
The young boy says he is more worried about being believed and trusted in the new place.
The young boy asks the young girl what she is thinking about.
She is thinking about what she left behind.
The young boy is thinking about today and what lies ahead.
The young girl is thinking about what she left behind.
They must both share the truth of why they left.
They must tell everything.
They must educate themselves.
They must learn to write.
They must write their history in a book and leave it for their children.

After our New Year in the new land, we are all split up.
After our New Year in our own country, we live together, work together, and plant rice together.
Our new land is very beautiful.
We have good houses.
We have cars and trucks.
The roads are paved.
But still we remember.
We think of home.
We remember the bird songs at sunrise.
We remember the grasshoppers jumping at dawn.
We remember the sound of heavy raindrops on leaves.
We remember the song of the male gibbon.
We remember the fruit trees…the pineapple, banana, and papaya.
We can still hear the owls cry to each other like we cry.
Where is the nraug cuas (creature of the night)? We can no longer hear him.
Where is the nraug cuas?

Orphan's Song

(Translation by Father Jean Mottin and Amy Catlin, published by UCLA Ethnomusicology Publications, Los Angeles, 90024, *Selected Reports In Ethnomusicology, Volume VI: Asian Music In North America*, 1984)

Note: This song was sung by a Blue Hmong woman in Northern Thailand, and illustrates how a song can encourage Hmong sympathy for orphaned children.

Son of theirs,
The poor orphan girl's mother and father
Are dead body and soul
And the poor orphan girl
Simply must close her mouth.
Son of theirs,
I feel like a dead hen,
A hen who does not know
How to come to a nest and lay eggs.

The poor orphan girl's mother and father
Are dead body and soul
And the poor orphan girl
Is being oppressed by others.

When she plows the fields
She is like a plowing ox
whose leg is broken.
The poor orphan girl's mother and father
Are dead body and soul
And the poor orphan girl
Will be without life or family.

When the poor orphan girl thinks she must go and pluck vegetables,
Then her people close the door loudly behind her.

When she returns
She peeps through the chinks in the walls
And sees them eating and sharing all the meat.

While they eat and share all the meat
They let her sleep curled up with the dogs and the pigs
Son of theirs.

They lie to her
Saying they have only eaten their share.
They send her to the stove to fetch her food
But when she looks for the meat, there is none,
And tears stream down her face.

When she sighs that she has no spoon,
But will manage simply with a plate,
How the people scold her,
Saying she has hidden her spoon...
Saying she has lost her spoon.

I am unhappy enough to die
When shall we meet again?
Perhaps in another life...

Nostalgic Hearts Fall to the Homeland

(By Kia Thao, translation by Amy Catlin, Khu Khang, and Cheu Thao, published by UCLA Ethnomusicology Publications, Los Angeles, 90024, *Selected Reports In Ethnomusicology, Volume VI: Asian Music In North America,* 1984)
Note: This song is an example of a contemporary text composed by a Minnesota Hmong band, recorded on an LP under the title Tsoom Hmoob (All The Hmong). As with this text, many contemporary songs address social issues.

All of us Hmong have new lives.
Before, when we were together in our country,
We saw everyone.
Now we have lost our country
And we have no land to control.

Think of our life before.
Now we are very lonely.
Tears fall from our eyes
Because we left parents and brothers
Behind in the jungle
Eating leaves and vines.

Now it is far away.
Here when we have morning sun
There is darkness for you.
Midday for us
Means midnight for you.

110

Please God, love us
So that we may meet soon.
You think of us
While we think of you.
We look at the sun
While you look at the moon.

Nau Blaii And Zie
as told by Mua Cha

(Recorded by David C. Graham in "Songs and Stories of the Ch'uan Miao", Washington, D.C. Smithsonian Miscellaneous Collection, 1954)

Once upon a time there was a poor orphan boy. When all the other young people put on their clothes and went to play the ball game at New Year's, he went around in rags. None of the girls wanted to play with him. He went home, took down his "geej" (which he played wonderfully well), and returned to where the young people were playing. He played and played beautifully, and, as he played, he danced. Zie, the youngest and most beautiful daughter, saw him and fell in love with him. She followed him home. He said: "Please go home. Your parents will never allow me to marry you".

When Zie went into his bedroom she found that he had a great many silver bowls, gold chopsticks, and other treasures (which the orphan boy is said to have stolen from the Monkey People in an earlier story in the sequence).

He said: "All these things are mine, not yours."

Zie decided to stay with him, but she did not become his real wife.

The orphan continued to play the "geej". He played it so well that the dead souls in heaven heard him and longed to have him come up to heaven to play for them. One beautiful morning, with a brilliant blue sky and the sun shimmering on the mountain peaks, Zie stood outside his door. She saw two butterflies fall from the sky, tumbling over and over each other until they reached the place where she stood. And lo, the two butterflies were two young men who said to her, "We want to take Nau Blaii up to heaven to play for us."

The orphan heard them and said: "How can I go to heaven? I cannot fly!"

The young men said: "That's easy, just put your head under our armpits."

The girl did not want the orphan to go. The two young men finally convinced her that it would only be until tomorrow, when they would bring him back to earth. So Nau Blaii put his head under their armpits. One moment, he heard a sound as though scratching the palm thatch of the roof - the next moment, he stood in heaven.

Nau Blaii played his "geej" to the souls in heaven. One of the girls in heaven fell in love with him. She would not let him return to the earth on the next day. He   111 tried to break away, but he could not. Every morning, he tried again and again to get away. Zie would hear the sound of the "geej" coming closer and closer, but instead of Nau Blaii appearing, the sound would fade away. Zie cried and cried. She decided to ask a wise shaman for help. He told her to take a spoon and hang it over the fireplace inside the house. He told her to spin the spoon around in her hands and to say: "May the heat from the spoon burn my love into Nau Blaii's heart." Now even though Nau Blaii in heaven was overwhelmed with a terrible longing for Zie, he could not escape.

In despair, Zie went back to the wise shaman and asked him what else she could do. "Go up to heaven and bring him back yourself," was the shaman's advice.

In those olden times, before men had become too evil, there was a road to heaven which has since become blocked. So Zie went to heaven. She looked everywhere, but could not find Nau Blaii.

Once again she returned to the shaman. He said: "Tomorrow morning I want you to stand by the road. You will see many horsemen pass. Wait until you see a miserable horse go by, and then grab onto the rider. He will be your love."

Zie did as she was advised. She waited and waited. Finally when she began to cry, she saw many horsemen ride by on fine, sleek horses. At the very far end of the column came a pitiful, dirty, miserable horse stumbling along. Zie remembered the shaman's words. She rushed out and grabbed the rider. It was, indeed, Nau Blaii. Zie and Nau Blaii went to a quiet place and talked and talked.

The heavenly girl, who had fallen in love with Nau Blaii, came to Zie and said: "You cannot have him, I want to marry him". What happened then is that the wise old men in heaven decided that the two girls should enter a competition with Nau Blaii as the prize. The competition was to see which girl was the most beautiful. The heavenly girl changed her clothes 3 times each day, wearing ever more lovely clothing, but she was still not as lovely as Zie, who was Nau Blaii's own true love. Finally, the elders in heaven gave Zie permission to marry Nau Blaii, which she did, and then they returned to earth.

Acknowledgements

The Hmong Natural Association of North Carolina, Incorporated, and the author, would like to gratefully acknowledge and thank the following institutions, corporations, and individuals for their financial support of this book:

-North Carolina Arts Council, Department Of Cultural Resources, and Mr. George Holt, Director, Folklife Section

-Mary Reynolds Babcock Foundation, Winston-Salem, North Carolina, and Mr. William L. Bondurant, Executive Director

-James G. Hanes Memorial Fund/Foundation, Winston-Salem, North Carolina, Mr. E. Ray Cope, Trustee

-The Blumenthal Foundation, Charlotte, North Carolina, Mr. Phillip Blumenthal, Trustee

-Marion Machine, Marion, North Carolina

-Dr. Paul T. Yun, M.D., Marion, North Carolina

-First Union National Bank, Marion, North Carolina

-First Presbyterian Church, Morganton, North Carolina, Rev. Homer T. Rickabaugh, Minister

-Garden Creek Baptist Church, Marion, North Carolina, Rev. Allen G. McKinney, Minister

-Dr. Allen W. Huffman, and Mrs. Barry G. Huffman, Hickory, North Carolina

We would additionally like to thank the following individuals who have contributed expertise, research help, moral support, and valuable criticism:

-Ms. Jean W. McLaughlin, North Carolina Arts Council

-Ms. Della Coulter, Folklife Specialist, North Carolina Arts Council

-Ms. Joanne Cubbs and the John Michael Kohler Arts Center, Sheboygan, Wisconsin

-Ms. Amy Catlin, Ph.D., Van Nuys, California

-Ms. Karen Hylnsky, Providence, Rhode Island

-Mr. Roger Early, Carolina Photo, Spruce Pine, North Carolina

-Mr. Ian Robertson, Warren Wilson College, Swannanoa, North Carolina

-Fairman and Kate Jayne, Sandy Mush Nursery, Leicester, North Carolina

-Mr. Robert Oldham, Celo Printing, Burnsville, North Carolina

-Ms. Sandra Epperson, McDowell Arts And Crafts Association, Marion, North Carolina

-Verne Stanford, Penland School Of Crafts, Penland, North Carolina

-Louise Todd-Cope, Penland, North Carolina

-Margaret Mott, Bowling Green, Ohio

-Joe Hollis and Rhea Rose Ormond, Celo, North Carolina

-Kue Chaw, Director, Hmong Natural Association Of N.C. Inc., and the following North Carolina Hmong: Mao Moua, Mai Kue, Mali Kue, Ma Lo, Lee Kue, Chou Kue, Lao Toua Lo, Xee Yang, Shaman Doua Kue, and a very special thanks to Maytong Kue and illustrator Thongsay Kue.